LONDON SOUVENIRS

LONDON SOUVENIRS

GEOFFREY S. FLETCHER

LONDON · GEORGE ALLEN & UNWIN LTD
RUSKIN HOUSE   MUSEUM STREET

First published in 1973

© George Allen & Unwin Ltd, 1973

ISBN 0 04 711005 8

Printed in Great Britain
in 12 point Fournier type
by William Clowes & Sons, Limited
London, Beccles and Colchester

Some portions of this book appeared in their original form in *The Daily Telegraph*, and I am happy to make the customary acknowledgements. The quotation from my book *London Overlooked* in 'Cupid in the Gallery' appears by kind permission of the Hutchinson Group.

'A Wreath for Armistice Day' and 'Cupid in the Gallery' are based on talks given in London.

Contents

Illustrations

A Wreath for Armistice Day

Today is Armistice Day. I mean, of course, the real day – not the pseudo one contrived to suit the convenience of modern Englishmen, bad in the hearts and mad in the head, concerned no longer with principle, but only with what will pay best. Now there was a time when men walking down Whitehall past the Cenotaph would uncover their heads. They used to do the same to passing funerals, and this I always thought ludicrous, yet the act of homage in Whitehall was right and true. Today, only the goggling tourists bestow a glance on it as part of their sightseeing programme.

What has all this got to do with an essay on London? Simply that London is changing for the worse, losing its character and appeal, shedding the civilising, life-giving qualities that made it the natural home not only for men of genius but also for those of none – for the innominate ones, generation after generation, who thought that little or nothing of interest or value existed outside the boundaries of the great city. When just now I used the words 'shedding and losing' I ought to have been more accurate. I ought to have said that its civilised values and character were being taken from it. Most of the changes are *not* inevitable. Sometimes insidiously, sometimes with arrogant effrontery, but always with ignorance and calculation, these things are thrust upon us, the virtually powerless, unthinking remainder. So I have decided that *you* – the users of this book – at least shall think over these things.

There is very little that we can do about it, though in the matter of the vandalistic destruction of fine old buildings and the atmospheric quarters of this and other cities, an informed public, able and willing to protest, can effect a certain amount of good on occasions – to check the rot, if not to cure it entirely. At the very least we ought to think clearly, to be fully aware of the nature of the co-ordinated, intricate campaign being waged against us and our environment by destroyers, bureaucrats, progressives and those simply out to make money. These changes, supposedly for our benefit, come thick and fast and in a variety of forms. The one thing they have in common is an arrogant disregard for what the rest of us really want (if it is only to be left alone) coupled with explanations designed to show up those who do protest as reactionaries, fools, ostriches, or an unimportant minority.

The process is being engineered over the whole of the country, assisted gratuitously by the degeneration of the race, the madness of modern Englishmen and the evil of the times. In London, particularly, not only the physical appearance but also the quality of life is degenerating at an alarming rate. This is not an isolated phenomenon but part of a

13

vast drift towards enervation and collapse, comparable to that which overtook the Romans when they lost the will to survive. The British Lion, once as formidable as magnamimous, has become as mean-spirited as decrepit. His sharp teeth, eroded by easy living and chemically preserved trash, have been replaced by ill-fitting National Health dentures. His cubs have long since deserted him, taking with them the lion's share of the provisions: they only trouble about his embarrassing existence when the need for further cadging arises.

A few friends in the zoo he still has left – the kangaroo, the beaver, the Dutch lion and, perhaps more doubtfully, the bald-headed eagle of America, but he fills them with despair, and they know his time is short. Those dark glasses of film star proportions he wears are no trendy notion out of Carnaby Street: he needs them right enough, for he is almost totally blind. As he peers from behind the bars the politicians and planners have built for him, he faces a disquieting and darkening landscape. The rivers of his ancient and beautiful domain are being slowly poisoned by the effluvia from a thousand industrial products which nobody needs. The very air, filled with a growing cacophony of noise, reeks with exhaust from the cars that multiply on the roads, making the life of the countryside a nightmare and urban living a hell. Moreover, besides interfering with ourselves, we are also interfering with the life of animals, creatures at least as important in the sight of God as ourselves, perhaps more.

On all sides rise hideous and soul-destroying buildings, some erected entirely without purpose, some with limitless possibilities of evil: offices where bureaucrats can work out more controls and manipulations, laboratories where defenceless animals are wickedly experimented on by half-mad scientists, hospitals where unborn babies (a new and up to date massacre of the innocents) are as lightly torn from the womb by Dr Jekyll and Sister Hyde as if God were dead or as cheerful and impotent as Father Christmas at the big stores. 'What would you like for Christmas?' asks God, peering from behind his false whiskers at the little Englishman. 'Why, man,' says the youngster, 'bigger aerodromes, faster cars, round the clock amusements, endless television, non-stop sex, longer holidays, increased excitement, more and more of everything!'

A thousand quack doctors are at hand, each with his sovereign remedy for the lion's complaint, though many of them have already contributed to his decline. 'London Bridge is obsolete, Covent Garden a bottleneck,' says the planning quack. 'What you need is a challenging, exciting architecture geared to the needs of the 1970s, '80s and beyond! Wider roads, pedestrian precincts, community centres, more and more controls!'

Here is the political quack. His bedside approach is *suavitur in modo*. He knows what must be done and so do his friends, as he assured the dupes at the time they were foolish enough to elect him, when he chatted up the housewives and kissed in their prams the specially disinfected babies. 'The lion's internal economy', says the medicine man, 'is certainly somewhat disordered and the pulse is erratic. A dose of North Sea gas – never mind whether he wants it or not – and the exercise of the metric and decimal systems will prove beneficial. We are encountering rough weather. The ship of state is not on an even keel, and we cannot see the light at the end of the tunnel. If we are to emerge from the wood we must all pull together. We must man the pumps, and stand shoulder to shoulder behind the man on the bridge. Only in that way shall we get out of the sidings and balance our books.' More and more laws, more and more policemen!

Before dropping this parable, I will just add one thing, as seriously as I know how: it hardly matters how incompetent are the quacks nor how fantastic their prescriptions for the patient is beyond hope of recovery.

Do not imagine that strange clothes, drugs and pop music, the worship of teen-agers as if they were a new and separate species that so frightens those of middle age, the increasing dirt and confusions of London, along with the tearing down of so much that made it fine, the horrors of contemporary life that lie just below its trendy, colour supplement surface and the contempt of administrators for individuals are all isolated facts. They are not. They are all symptoms of the same disease, a death wish that has pursued the ineffectual English since 1945 – the widespread decline in standards, the lack of will to cultivate and maintain civilised values – a disease accelerated by national exhaustion, laziness, ignorance and apathy in the face of the plans by authoritarians to reduce us to final and abject slavery.

The cumulative effect of all this on London has been disastrous. Hampstead, not so many years since still notable for its peace and village-like seclusion, has become a noisy, petrol-perfumed hell – crazy with traffic in the morning and evening rush hours, when you cannot cross Heath Street for the belching, grinding, bumper to bumper cars, and at weekends hideous beyond description. When I lived in Chelsea twenty years or so ago it was still in large parts of it recognisably the Chelsea of Whistler and Carlyle, however untalented and bogus their artistic and literary descendants. You found peace and contentment in its old, cloister-like squares. The sounds of Cheyne Walk were confined to the rustling of autumn leaves, or perhaps the sighs of Victorian ghosts, and the occasional hooting of tugs and steamers. Today, no one could go there to contemplate unless he were prepared to be asphyxiated by the fumes and deafened by the roars of non-stop lorries on their way to Wandsworth. The Kings Road was once one of the most pleasant places in which to spend an afternoon, strolling and window gazing at a variety of shops, old and new, with here and there a nice and slightly dotty old lady, left over from the Chelsea of John or Henry James: now it has become unspeakably trendy and tedious, full of with-it boutiques from end to end, staffed with those bearded, bespectacled hipsters, students and freaks who are beginning to bore me to distraction – and no Chelsea Palace Music Hall bill, warm and crummy, to round off the day!

As to the shameful, uneducated things that have been done to the City of London, both by commercial developers and their architects and by those administrators who ought to know better, I cannot write without anger. These destructions, this futile creation of worthless matter unworthy of the name of architecture, would not have occurred in the city of Paris, where things are managed very differently, to the lasting benefit of its citizens and its visitors. I know and love Paris very well, and there are times – times increasing in frequency and intensity – when I am ashamed to be English. But Paris is a city of tremendous vistas, and London was a city not of wide boulevards nor magnificent distances, but of courtyards and narrow places and quarters such as Soho, full of well-used Georgian houses, declining either gracefully or picturesquely into old age; gas lamps and humble, unpretending streets with the great churches and public buildings interposed here and there, all with a characteristic individualism and variety. The result was that London was both grand and homely, splendid yet humane.

This harmony has now been disrupted, the skyline made hideous and the unique feeling of domesticated grandeur destroyed. What we are getting in exchange is the soulless London of the planners – those who know what is best for us – the London of the advertising men who press on us an insatiable appetite for possession, for owning things we don't really need; the London of bad food, sloppily served at high prices in restaurants where they want us to move on as soon as possible; the London of inhuman blocks of flats, of dreary offices staffed by suburban commuters who take no interest in London as a creative place and who possess neither the money nor the desire to make the long suburban journey to sample its amenities, its galleries, theatres and parks.

My notebooks, my published books on London and my files of newspaper drawings and articles are a factual record of decline, part, as I have said, of a nation-wide retreat and disengagement from all that makes for the supremacy of the individual, for all conditions of fine and wholesome life. Think over all this. But do not think that in general – in general – the process can be stopped. It cannot. It is irremediable, irresistible, irreversible as long as we continue to allow ourselves to be under the power of others. You may not have been aware that anything was seriously wrong or, being aware, may have preferred not to ponder on it. That past master of the hallucinatory speech, Stanley Baldwin, once justified his brainwashing technique on the grounds that a general audience was imperfectly prepared to follow a close argument. I would go further and add that nowadays the whole nation (if you will allow a generalisation) is not merely imperfectly prepared to follow an argument, it is entirely averse to the labour of any kind of thinking. We don't want to know, we don't want to be involved. 'Don't look', we say to ourselves, 'and it (whatever *it* is) will go away.' Meanwhile, more of everything!

When we read of new outrages on the homes of Londoners – the monstrous taking away of people's homes for motorways, aerodromes and the rest of it or the knocking down of areas supposedly substandard – we may commiserate, *but we do nothing about it.* It is always someone else who is affected. Besides, these things are always accompanied by propaganda. We are always told that such manipulations are in the interests of the public. What public? Who are the public? It does not, in fact, exist. There is no public.

There is no society. There are only individuals. Those who are unfortunate enough to live in the path of a projected scheme (never, by the way, any of the bureaucrats themselves) are certainly members of the bureaucrat's public, and surely the robbery of their homes can hardly be of benefit to *them*. In brief, the term is one that cannot be precisely defined: it is like the quibbles of Plato's *Socratic Discourses*: how many stones are there in a heap? The thing is an abstraction, and so is the public, for there are many publics, almost as many as there are Englishmen, and some of them overlap. I am part of the public of the man who makes Swiss rolls; if he reads my books, he is part of mine; both of us are part of the butcher's, and so on. We are *all*, however, part of the official planner's public and perhaps of the commercial developer's too. But in the final scrutiny, the term is highly misleading, and the rascals who use it know this perfectly well.

We may not have much hope of saving London and its adjoining areas, but at least we ought not to let them get away with it, without reasoned protest, without thought. Rather more than that, we ought to send them packing – now. We would certainly do so, but for our massive laxity and our inability to understand the signs of the times – what the revolting welfare state and social engineering is leading to. People have heard so much about the permissive society – so called – that by mere repetition they may have come to believe in it. But we should understand that this is only one of the many bogus beliefs now in circulation, largely the creation of journalists and those pseudo-scientific talkers who plague us on the wireless and the television. What existence it has in the real world is confined to a small and quite unimportant sector, as powerless as the rest of us, and what permissiveness it has can be cut short at any time by those whose business it is to manipulate us. There is no harm in allowing us to think that there are fewer and fewer restraints, for it is, in fact, no more than a convenient diversion, a smoke screen.

When 'the powers that be' are ready to take people's land and homes away for yet another unwanted aerodrome, to forcibly depopulate some area of this city where people have lived for generations, when they are ready to propel us into a new war, what then of the permissive society? You will find it has disappeared overnight. I could give off-hand a dozen or more instances of the calculated spoilation of London (to say nothing of the vast destructions elsewhere) – a movement, as I have said, that is only part of a complex situation. Here a fine old terrace is threatened, there a London village, elsewhere a whole area. Sometimes objections lead to a public inquiry, so-called. But the fact is that the 'public', apart from those immediately concerned, is but thinly represented at these affairs. Most Londoners have neither the time nor the special knowledge, even if they had the interest, and I am very confident that those who hold such inquiries are very well aware of this; in short, they know that we are dummies, as futile in point of action as the waxworks of Madame Tussaud.

I will cite just one example. There was a large area of fine, solidly built Victorian terraces grouped around a North London Square. They were in the Georgian tradition, though, being later, were less refined, and needed only a certain amount of plumbing and interior modernisation. But the local council decided they were slums, a deliberate perversion of the truth. They had in mind a most frightful modern development, designed to raise their prestige and to house a few more people to the acre. They compulsorily acquired various properties in and around the area, and allowed them to decay, thus creating artificially the conditions they pretended actually to exist – an old trick, which, however, always works. There was an inquiry at which I appeared on behalf of those whose homes were threatened. The council had secured the services of a famous Q.C. I shudder to think of the fee marked on his brief. The defenders were obliged to do the same. Now, apart from the outrage of people having to defend their own homes for *any* reason, the monstrous audacity of the thing in *any* light, the residents had not only to pay for their counsel, his junior and what else, but also through the rates contribute to the costs of their adversary, an adding of injury to injury. Needless to say, the homes of the attackers were not themselves in jeopardy – they never are!

Is it possible that we shall halt the destruction of London before all that made it a great civilised city has gone for good? Is it possible that, in the larger context, we shall continue to think of ourselves as living comfortably in a right little, tight little island, where the unavoidable strains of a complicated life are catered for by compromise and adjustment – that, taken as a whole, things are pretty well? Are we likely to wake up to reality and see the true nature of the experiments being made on us, ones without real redress? I will give you my answer. England is destined to become a living hell, and English life will be overtaken by horrors which are even now peering in at the window – a vast regimentation; secularisation and its companion, unbelief; total mechanisation; the scientific control of human beings by means of force, propaganda and advertising: these are only a few of the life-destroying things now quietly assembling for the *coup de grâce*.

You may say I am pessimistic. At least you cannot say that you have not been warned. As long as authoritarianism of whatever sort is allowed to continue, so long will the quality of life be eroded. There are only two main divisions of Englishmen: the authoritarians, who cannot live without dominating others, and we who abjectly permit them to do so. The former, though proliferating, are still in the minority, but they have gained the victory of the weak over the strong. If we at least become aware of the monstrous absurdity of allowing men and women of our own race to have dominion over us, we might decide it were well to require them to pack their bags and be gone.

You might ask two questions. First, what business of mine is all this? What qualifications as an artist have I to serve me in such matters? Just this: that it is the business of the artist to see with the inward eye as much as with the outward, to reflect on the nature as well as on the appearance of things. If the artist – in the fullest meaning of the word –

does not speak out for that liberty which is the right of all creatures whatever, who shall?

You might also wonder what constructive suggestions I can offer in the way of amelioration. There I can make no answer. I do not believe there is an answer in the existing state of things. As I have remarked, I believe the patient to be dead. That is why I can only offer a wreath for Armistice Day.

Cupid in the Gallery

The following pages are the substance of a discourse on the Bedford which I gave at the Holborn Library. It was a sentimental occasion, for in the audience were a number of old-timers (senior citizens in the ridiculous, nauseating jargon of the welfare state) who were present at Marie Lloyd's 50th birthday celebrations held at the Bedford in 1920, when the junketings went on to a late hour. The reminiscences of a man who can say 'I was there' are always interesting – as interesting as a beautiful lie, sometimes; they have the attraction for us that the memories of an ammonite might have, could he but tell us about the dinosaurs: for history is not always an agreed fiction, as Napoleon made it out to be.

The vast and unwieldy area now called Camden is particularly rich in theatrical tradition, especially in St Pancras where many local theatres have come and gone. The next on the list might well be the Camden Theatre, built by Sprague and opened by Ellen Terry in 1900, for it stands on what developers call a 'plum' site. Not far from the Lecture Room was the Holborn Empire, demolished when a wreck to make way for the western extension of the Edwardian offices of the Pearl Assurance. This extension, carried out in the same Edwardian Baroque, gives, of course, no clue to the present-day wanderer that a great and famous music-hall ever stood there. But it was at the Holborn that George Lashwood, last of the Lion Comiques, sang the praises of the London tramcar – of the felicity attendant on a ride on its upper deck. It was at the Holborn that the career of George Barnes came to an end, apart from a finale devoted to collecting empty glasses at a Westcliff pub.

Camden is rich in theatrical history, but the Bedford was supreme. When we tire of exciting theatres – theatres in the round, theatres with apron stages, experimental theatres, audience participation and so on – we can console ourselves by thinking that the defunct music-hall was one of the few authentic art forms originated by the English, and that we had the inspiration to create an architecture – typified by the Bedford – in which to set it forth.

I have taken my title from one of the many paintings done by Walter Richard Sickert of the Bedford. Sickert produced more pictures of the Bedford than any other music-hall – at least five of the Old Bedford and at least four of what was at first called the New Bedford, besides several drawings, as well he might, for the Bedford – both Bedfords – was the most beautiful music-hall in London. And now it has gone. Some few months ago the last traces of it were razed to the ground after standing, or rather crumbling for a decade and a half, abandoned to wind and weather, a refuge for tramps and drop-outs, melancholy, mournful.

So it seems not unreasonable in an Arts Festival to pronounce a funeral oration over it, at the same time deploring the chronic shortsightedness which allowed it to decay when it could so easily have been saved to delight future generations. Not, I admit, to function in its proper capacity as a music-hall, for the music-hall as an institution – a means of entertainment – is as dead as Queen Anne, and the attempts to revive it as feeble and futile; but to have kept the building intact for the beauty of its interior – its merits as a piece of theatre design – would have been an end in itself. One would have thought that, seeing how great the contribution made by the music-hall in general was to London life, at least one of its fine late-Victorian halls might be allowed to survive, if only as a memorial of things that had been – like its churches.

It was not so: London has an ugly habit of giving short shrift to its favourites of yesterday, human as well as architectural, doesn't want to know them when it tires of them and has passed on to newer toys, in this case cars and television, all the things that gloss over our emptiness, restlessness and craving for novelty.

From its obscure and at times ribald origins in the supper and song saloons and the pubs and taverns providing a musical entertainment, the London music-hall became in the course of a lifetime a new and unique art form, fostering brilliant talents and a rich, lively and florid architecture; it existed solely for the entertainment of the people, from whose lowly environment it offered a means of escape; it depended on the suffrage of the people, and when they withdrew their support, the music-hall collapsed. It recorded, as on a sensitised plate, the ups and downs, squalid or comic, of life in this great city; it held a mirror up to the Londoner, enabling him to laugh at himself when there was nothing else to laugh at. And when he had forgotten how to laugh, how to enjoy himself... why, then it was Exodus!

The first Bedford – the Old Bedford of Sickert's *Cupid in the Gallery* – was built in what was then called Grove Street, off Camden High Street, in 1861. Its first owner was R. C. Thornton, who himself opened the hall in September 1861. A Mr Wilson was installed as manager. After passing through several changes of ownership, the Bedford became the property of Harry Hart, who did much to establish the Bedford as one of the leading halls. The sixties was a period of great expansion for the music hall: new buildings appeared in all parts of London in response to the demand for this essentially democratic entertainment. Sickert's paintings of the Old Bedford, including the one I have mentioned, *Cupid in the Gallery* (now in Ottawa, with another version in Liverpool), give us fascinating glimpses of its interior – brass railings, rich plasterwork, mirrors reflecting tobacco smoke, feathered bonnets and titfers. In common with the Canterbury in Westminster Bridge Road, the Bedford had a sliding roof for ventilation on summer nights. Sickert appeared on the scene in the halcyon days of the halls, when the audience still sat at tables served by waiters, exchanging pleasantries or otherwise with the chairman, and ready to offer criticism in the shape of rotten fruit if a 'turn' failed to please. All the great stars of the period – great because they had personality and style – appeared at the Bedford – Bessie Bellwood, Vesta Victoria, Katie Lawrence. They came from the same humble backgrounds as their audiences, which is why they knew them so well. Marie Lloyd gave her first performance at the Old Bedford about 1886. It became her favourite hall. She took over from Little Dot Hetherington a song (also sung by Nellie Power) that perhaps more than any other expresses the special flavour of the halls, 'The Boy I love is up in the Gallery'.

When I came to include a sequence in the Bedford's ruined interior in my film *The London Nobody Knows*, the camera swept round the ruined auditorium, breaking off to contrast its woebegone appearance with stills from Sickert's pictures, one of which was the painting of Little Dot Hetherington singing this song – a picture painted in 1889. Seen reflected in a mirror, she points her finger at a stage-struck Johnnie in the gallery. And I had the song sung again on the soundtrack as background music, bringing a breath of life to that deserted and stricken interior:

> The Boy I love is up in the Gallery
> The Boy I love is looking down at me
> There he is – can't you see him, waving of his hankeycher
> As merry as a robin that sings on a tree.

Noctes Ambrosianae! Nights of gladness! What were we thinking of to let the music-hall die?

Well, the old Bedford was burned down in 1899. With the new century came a new Bedford, also drawn and painted by Sickert, who delighted in its caryatid figures – a pair on each side, above the stage boxes. Again there was charming plasterwork in cream and blue and gold, the plush was blue and the draperies, held aloft by those wonderful caryatides, were blue, and there were mirrors once more and gas brackets, and a splendid bar, for, by this date, the tables had been banished from the auditorium. The style of the new Bedford was very close to the work of Frank Matcham, as might be expected, for it was designed by Bertie Crewe, Matcham's assistant and pupil. The exterior was not very exciting: in all the halls the interior was all-important, calling for exuberant detailing on the part of the architect and much skill on the part of the plasterer.

This music-hall baroque or rococo (sometimes the two are combined or both might be amalgamated with ornamental details vaguely suggestive of Eastern or Moorish styles – it hardly mattered provided the style was opulent enough) had a similar aim to that of the contemporary pub interior – to create a temporary escape from reality. Ritualistic religion, booze and popular songs, comic, pathetic or patriotic, were the chief anodynes for the lower classes. Don't imagine the Victorians were the only ones to construct escape ladders – the need for escapism is quite as pressing today – the means to

22

effect it have changed, that is all, and today take the form of cars, televisions, drugs, a spurious interest in the so-called underprivileged and in sexual deviations. What is specially striking about music-halls is that, though the architecture was 'escapist', the songs and the humour were essentially down to earth.

Sickert painted several upright canvases and produced at least one etching of the new Bedford's interior: these date from the Great War years. In these, the audience is distinctly more genteel. The billycock hat brigade who packed the gallery and peered through its brass rails in a haze of tobacco smoke – the Gods whose knowledge of life (apart from the London pavements) was derived solely from the pages of *Tit Bits* – have gone: most of them had been butchered by the politicians and generals on the Somme and the Marne.

This change corresponds to a shift in the character of the music-hall itself: it was also moving towards something less robust, less vigorous, towards what was known as 'variety'. I haven't time to analyse for you the exact implications of this change of emphasis. Simply grasp the fact that the music-hall was an essentially popular art, with the majority of the stars coming from the same background as their audiences. It was created by the common people of an industrialised society, and variety was not. The difference can be gauged by the fact that the Bedford ended up by styling itself 'The Family Theatre' – a long way, you see, from the old free and easy. It had become respectable: *tempora mutantur et nos mutamur in illis*. The BBC played a part in its history when they wanted a theatre as a studio, and they took it for a time, producing music-hall type shows with a troupe of girls of the TV Topper genre brought down. But this was at a comparatively recent date, and I am anticipating myself.

The Bedford had all the leading stars of the 1920s and 1930s on its bills, but the one chiefly to be remembered – the one who truly belonged to the music hall stage – was Marie Lloyd. Indeed, the Bedford's most memorable occasion was on February 12th, 1920 – Marie Lloyd's 50th birthday. From contemporary accounts we can get something of its flavour – the stage banked on all sides with flowers, the bouquets, the enthusiasm of the audience, the other old-timers such as Joe Elvin and Arthur Roberts, the champagne. She collapsed with the excitement, coming on top of continual overwork, private misfortunes and failing health: two years later she was dead. The audience were unaware that her staggerings on stage were the real thing. They thought it was the stage business, the simulated drunkenness that accompanied 'One of the Ruins that Cromwell Knocked About a Bit'. She was worn out and broken down, but her work was as good as ever. She had a new song, 'My old man said follow the van', one of the character songs that enabled her to use her Cockney accent and style. But though such songs could still be composed and understood – for the midnight flit which it celebrated was still a flourishing institution in the early 1920s – they and the old Cockney life were things of the past, and so was the music-hall, if we are truthful: for the fact is, though its full meaning was not yet generally understood, the Great War had precipitated the English into the twentieth century, an age of mass entertainment, mass manipulation, and in this climate, the sublime selfishness of the individualist – the condition that produced the greatest art of past times – found no encouragement and no favour.

At the end of the last war, when in my student days my Bedford adventures began, the 'turns' there were sometimes poor to the point of being appalling, but many of the old stars who could still hold an audience appeared there – George Robey, for instance. This was before such impresarios as Don Ross got the idea of gathering up such remaining practitioners as his wife, Gertie Gitana, and G. H. Elliott and putting them on the road once again, though there had been 'Thanks for the Memory' type shows before the war, starring old-timers who had survived into the 1930s. I will say this for the Bedford – it seldom touched such rock bottom, twentieth-rate touring shows as did Collins's at Islington, whose shows in its last days reached an all-time low. Not that I minded much what the show was – the Bedford's plasterwork of caryatides, proscenium arch, garlands, ribands, bay leaves (or were they supposed to be olive leaves – this ubiquitous leafage of the music-hall?), masks and what not were entertainment enough, either catching the lights unexpectedly from the stage, fitful gleams of gold here and there in the dark, or seen in full illumination when the house lights were on. I used to go up in the mornings, during rehearsals, and then again in the evenings in the gallery. Those high-stepping floosies in fishnet stockings – how disenchanting they were when they turned up in their headscarves, fresh (or not so fresh) from their theatrical digs, as unlike their same selves of the evening as possible. Thirty years in the chorus, and never dropped a spangle!

The Bedford always had a strong *pièce de résistance*, often of a religious turn, one never quite knew why, and the troupe of floosies would come on dressed as nuns, with the fishnet stockings showing below the habit, to sing Ave Maria in the beam of the limelight . . . oh yes, they had a turn for art, high art, at the Bedford. Nor were they backward when patriotic sentiment was wanted. Like Gilbert's Wandering Minstrel, they had patriotic ballads cut and dried, and a low comic, who might also be the juggler in the same bill under another name, could bring on roars of applause by making the V-sign, Churchill fashion.

Many of the drawings I made then have somehow disappeared, though I have kept a few – not, however, those in the library's collection, which were made later when the theatre had become disused after futile attempts to interest the locals in Victorian melodrama and in Shakespeare during the late 1940s and early '50s. By the time the Bedford sequence I have spoken of (with James Mason stirring the debris with his umbrella) came to be made in 1968, the place had become a dangerous structure. In fact there was much difficulty in getting consent to take the actor and camera team in there at all, but eventually permission was granted, and the place cleaned up sufficiently to allow filming to be done. A few years before, however, in 1963, I determined to make at least a small number of drawings while it was still possible. My description written at the time for my Hutchinson book, *London Overlooked*, still seems vivid and evocative, and I quote it here by permission of the publishers.

'Strong nerves and determination are necessary for the solitary exploration of the derelict London halls. Apart from the risk of falling masonry or the breaking of one's neck on ruined staircases, there are the other discomforts incidental to such explorations in the shape of tramps, dead or alive or with one foot in the grave, and rats. Moreover, left alone in these places where the plaster masks smile down on scenes of absolute decay, one has a disagreeable knack of recalling various stories of odd happenings in London theatres – the ghostly hands at the St James's or the noises and sinister opening doors Lew Lake used to talk about at Collins's. I recently revisited the Bedford after the lapse of several years on a day matched to the purpose, one of lowering dark clouds and heavy rain. The sudden view of the ruined auditorium from back-stage was infinitely melancholy and depressing. I picked my way gingerly across the stage where great gaps in the slippery boards disclosed a depth of several feet of filthy water in the mezzanine below the joists. The safety curtains hung in shreds, flapping eerily, like the banner of a hopeless cause in the wind that moaned through that deserted place. Rain poured steadily through a hole in the ceiling . . . not an elaborate ceiling, like the Metropolitan's, but a simple, elegant arrangement of mouldings and plain surfaces. . . . The seats had long disappeared, so had the charming art nouveau caryatides, all but one which still supported the plaster draperies of the adjoining box. Those solid looking nymphs, columns and archivolts were nothing but plaster and jute: time had dealt severely with their pretensions and shown them to be an elegant sham.

On the floor, among the crumbling plaster ornaments, lay a long-dead Christmas tree. Tramps had taken shelter in the music-hall, leaving their stinking rags on the floor, along with their excreta. Down and outs had evidently occupied the boxes – possibly the only time they had ever indulged in the luxury – and flies, surely the least fastidious of the creatures of God (less than men and women, even) crawled over the droppings.

The plaster was almost gone from the fronts of the gallery and circle, showing the fireproof construction underneath, but the supporting figures on the proscenium arch, one each side of the coat of arms, were intact, as were the four cupids, two each side above the boxes. I explored the dark staircases and passages by the light of a small torch; from the gods, the derelict interior appeared even more melancholy than from below. Suddenly, turning round in the dark, I saw the outline of a figure moving about behind a door in the gallery, and felt my pulse missing a beat . . . several beats. Fortunately, it was my own figure, reflected in the glass of a door in the gloom, but it was an undesirable sensation while it lasted. Empty theatres are always full of strange sounds – muffled footfalls, whisperings – and to listen to the moaning of the wind, the beating of the rain and one's own heart in the darkened gallery of an abandoned music-hall, where doors mysteriously open and shut, is not pleasant. I wondered if, after all, I was not alone – if I had company besides the ginger cat I saw stalking across the stage: visitors who ought to be resting. I thought of Belle Elmore. The murder of Belle Elmore was a crime with a complete music-hall background. She appeared at the Bedford – this Bedford – on this stage – quite often – a throw-away turn. She was a Jewess, fond of jewellery, and Crippen, her husband – that wonderfully sinister Crippen with the heavy moustache and fishlike eyes – gave her plenty. Marie Lloyd recognised some of the pieces being worn by Ethel Le Neve (and, by the way, Ethel Le Neve was still alive a year or two ago – I don't know whether she has now joined her former lover in Paradise) at a variety artists' ball, and she reported her suspicions to Scotland Yard.'

In its heyday as a living music-hall, other artists besides Sickert (but mostly those under his influence) were drawn towards the Bedford, its audiences and its *fin de siècle* finery – Spencer Gore, for instance, and other members of the Camden Town, later the London, Group. But the magic worked only for Sickert – or to reverse this aphorism – only Sickert worked the magic. Their drawings and paintings are useful as records, but they fail to come to life. The Bedford was also recorded in one or two films – not, of course, deliberately, with a definite object in view, as in my film – but simply as a theatre interior, at once suitable and convenient in the days when British film producers (often, I admit, oppressed by shoe-string budgets) seldom used other than London locations whatever the script called for – an economy that left little scope for imaginative directors and none at all for those who valued authenticity! In providing a background for these film and television producers, the Bedford was thereby feeding the hand that was biting it – a reversal of the proverb. So, what with one thing and another – the disappearance of the genuine Londoner who remained true to his part of the town, the influence of American ideas – for we always get the worst of these – the cinema, silent and talking, television and the complex changes that accompanied the organisation of the modern welfare state – humourless, mass produced, mendicant, processed, greedy yet purposeless – what with one thing and another, I say, such places as the Bedford could not survive, any more than the type of great and extraordinary artistes who appeared on its stage. Now the Bedford is only a space, a site to be developed, soon to be covered over, in Camden High Street. As I was making a colour drawing of the exterior, two girls passed, looked at the disused Bedford, and one asked the other, 'What was a music-hall, anyway?' And the other (both were about sixteen) said, 'It was a place where they used to sing.'

No better epitaph could be devised, full of sadness and perhaps a touch of unconscious irony.

Our revels are now ended: These our actors,
As I foretold you, were all spirits, and
Are melted into air, into thin air:
And, like the baseless fabric of this Vision
The cloud-capped towers, the gorgeous palaces,
The solemn temples, the great globe itself,
Yea, all which it inherit, shall dissolve
And, like this insubstantial pageant faded,
Leave not a rack behind.

Barter
Street
Gallery

ANDREW BLOCK PRINTS

BARTER STREET, BLOOMSBURY

This Side of Paradise

The City of God is, I imagine, much like the London of forty years ago, though, instead of petering out among semis and potted meat factories, it goes on without end. All our dog friends are there, cocking their legs against the trees of its crystal pavements – much to the delight of St Francis – and celestial trams advertising Hudsons Soap and Epps Cocoa glide down the leafy thoroughfares past secondhand bookshops in uncountable numbers, full of rare finds. There the friendless old men who haunt the Bloomsbury bookshops surely find that the Proprietor gives them all they want for nothing. This is because He is well aware that the old men, hard-up students and clergymen are still up to their old incorrigible tricks. Long before they enter a shop, He knows that they will try to slip books feloniously into the pockets of their spiritual shabby macs, and wishes to spare them all embarrassment.

This side of Paradise, however, less satisfactory arrangements prevail, particularly in present-day London, where worthwhile books are harder to drop on and bargains almost – but not quite – a thing of the past. Twenty odd years ago when I was at University College one could pick up the most fantastic bargains; first editions of Ruskin that now fetch £20 could be had for a bob or so. I bought the Moxon Tennyson illustrated by the Pre-Raphaelites for 3s 6d from Eric Blundell's shop in Marchmont Street, where the owner, his wife and the tortoise-shell cat were all book lovers with a soft spot for impecunious students and never minded if they didn't buy. From the same delightful source came Walter Crane books at three bob and Berwick's *Quadrupeds*, second edition, for seventeen shillings and sixpence. To reflect on these things gives one a queer, unsettling feeling of having come out of the Ark.

There is no more exquisite pleasure than that of pouncing on a secondhand book, except of reading it with the attendant joys of fags, wine and a coal fire. In doing so, I delight in thinking of previous owners and wondering what they were like. In my first edition of Ruskin's *Elements of Drawing* is the dedication 'To Selina Moore, with her Father's Love 1857'. You must have been very keen on drawing, Selina, for Papa to have bought you Mr Ruskin's rather difficult treatise! Or was there perhaps a young man in the case, causing a degree of moodiness and dislocation to an orderly household, and Papa bought the book for its medicinal value as a cooling agent? I wonder as, in my imagination, I see you bending over your mahogany box of watercolours and camels' hair pencils in the drawing room when the gas is lit?

Another book, *The Great Metropolis*, a collection of engravings with text by a

Grub Street hack, has this inscription: 'To Master B. for his exemplary conduct and attention to his lessons during his Father's absence at the Great Exhibition 1851'. I know you, too, Master B., and a precious little swot you were! You were the original do-gooder and of the Gradgrind persuasion; you sat mugging up your bally Anabasis and Gallic Wars during that long hot summer when you should have been out in the garden, where the blackbird and thrush were praising their Creator in the apple trees, or else you ought to have been sticking hat pins in the maid-of-all-work's bottom!

One of my books has just returned from restoration by an expert; I could no longer bear the water stains on the cover. Having disinterred it for two bob, after years of searching, I walked for miles in order to gloat in private. My way took me along a deserted canal. Suddenly, round a bend, I heard the sound of splashing water. In the shadow of a bridge, there was someone drowning. I threw the book down, and, after a titanic struggle, fished out an old man. I was covered in evil smelling mud; so was the book. Therefore, I could hardly credit my ears when, after getting the water out of his lungs, he accused me of interfering with his intention of committing suicide and said that to carry it out was no crime. As I walked away, I replied, 'You suicides are all alike, and never think of the mess it entails on others. In your case, you have committed a far greater crime than attempted suicide. You have caused to be splashed with mud a first edition of Eastlake's *History of the Gothic Revival*, and for that there can be no forgiveness.'

The prices at the London book auctions nowadays give a clue to the changed times. People are evidently buying for investment, even in seventeenth-century books of divinity, once bought only to furnish the shelves of Philistine tycoons and never on any account read by any human being. Charing Cross Road, once a perfect Klondyke, has not yielded (as far as I am concerned) a rare find for years but Cecil Court, former home of the film industry in the earliest silent days, is still on the active list and its shops worth a morning of anyone's time. Farringdon Road market, though a shadow of its old self, is by no means barren, and the Bloomsbury bookshops are as promising – or nearly so – as ever. There is an excellent bookshop at the back of Cartwright Gardens, in Burton Street, in what used to be a curious old cobbler's shop, and the one in my illustration, famous for prints as well as books, in Barter Street. All these, a few out of many, are good earths for bookworms: try them for size.

A Trumpet in Zion

The little boy in the T-shirt playing a tin trumpet in an alley off Old Montague Street was, I thought, symbolic, and I told him so – before he took to his heels. There he stood, unconscious of its terrible history, in the heart of the old Ghetto, blowing a trumpet in Zion, a latter-day Joshua, commanding the walls to fall at the sound of brazen instruments. Had I been making a film, he would have been a gift from the gods.

Though Old Montague Street is part of a large area scheduled for redevelopment, it is as yet only disappearing piecemeal. Much of the old, superannuated property stands eyeless and empty. Premises are being boarded up at intervals along the shabby, odiferous street, and the old open-air shop where the elderly Jewish woman sold smoked and salted fish has gone to make way for a temporary car park. In Black Lion Yard, too, where for generations East Enders came to buy engagement rings on Sunday mornings, are ominous signs of the shape of things to come. I have always been attached to Old Montague Street and its broken-down environs, as was an earlier and even greater criminal, Jack the Ripper. But even he has been overtaken by time and change, and only recently the house in Hanbury Street where Jack despatched the second of his prostitute victims has disappeared. Therefore, visit Whitechapel now for a living slice of the Victorian East End!

Enter Old Montague Street from Osborn Street, a locality once noted for its Russian restaurants, including the Warsaw at No. 32. Anarchists and Nihilists formed the chief clientele of these places, and among them was Peter the Painter and his guntoting accomplices of the Houndsditch murders and the siege of Sidney Street. After the Spitalfield Huguenots came the Irish, en route, if they could make it, for the New World. Next, in the terrible 1880s came the Jews, fleeing from persecution in Rumania, Latvia, Poland, Russia – nearly all arriving penniless at the London Docks, with the inevitable address written in English on a bit of paper. Those who made the grade moved off to the promised land of Maida Vale. Most of them starved in the sweat shops devoted to slop tailoring and other industries then carried on in unspeakable conditions. But indigent or not, they all set up their chevras or synagogues here and there in dark alleys, held their festivals and praised the Lord of Hosts.

> They wandered in the wilderness in a desert way;
> They found no city of habitation.
> Hungry and thirsty,

OLD MONTAGUE STREET, WHITECHAPEL

Their soul fainted in them.
Then they cried unto the Lord in their trouble,
And he delivered them out of their distresses.
He led them also by a straight way
That they might go to a city of habitation.

And they had their record, those fugitives of the teeming East End, in the strangely moving, shrewdly observed, at times sentimental, novel by Israel Zangwill, *The Children of the Ghetto*. This all but forgotten book is full of the smells and sounds, the felicities and backslidings of that curfewless Ghetto. Though dated, it is vivid, real and compelling. But you must not expect it to throw much light on the mystery of the Hebrew people: that no man can do, or if he could, then the explanation would be more baffling than the riddle, as it would be with the Irish or their oriental counterparts, the people of India.

Though fine Jewish heads are still to be seen, Indians and other dark-skinned races have now almost taken over. The quarter has become a melting pot of all the races out of Babel. Sometimes you feel the edgy, knifelike, nightmarish atmosphere is growing unbearable, even without the meths men. Only recently I saw a Negro spit at a Jewish shopkeeper – surely a nice problem for the Race Relations Board? Such ugly lapses apart, the street is wonderfully evocative. Crates of fowls arrive; their squawking and their feathers alike float out of the slaughterhouse, whence men in bloody aprons and gumboots emerge periodically to slake their thirst at the Kosher corner café. Everything round here is Kosher, and, when it's not, it's Taj Mahal. A West Indian looks in at the carnage and says, 'Kill, kill, kill, nothin' but killin' de world over.'

Jazz oozes out of the clubs, decorative Indian women in bright silks glide up and down. Along the pavements is a perspective of silent Orientals and Pakistanis – as silent as the cast-iron bollards.

Pauline Terrace, of grey Victorian brick, complete with Gothic ornament, is utterly squalid. The stench from rotting food and junk cast down the area is almost too stimulating; ferns have gained a foothold in the walls, and a willowherb blooms from a crack in a windowsill, proving the persistence of life in extreme conditions. Observe it all, and end up in Black Lion Yard, where lived the murdered Leon Beron, a receiver, probably, for Peter the Painter's gang. You will see a most interesting relic – the remains of the cowkeeper's yard. Milking cows were kept in the East End as recently as the late 1930s. On the rotting doors of the yard are the words

J. D. & J. Evans, Cowkeepers

and an inscription in Hebrew indicating that the milk is Kosher. The shippons, though decayed, are intact; everything is decayed and grass and ragwort grow between the granite setts.

Not everyone shares my love of the obsolete and ruinous; still, it is yesterday's witness to a vanished life. What's more, my luck was in, for I love old bottles, too, and I found and purloined a pair of beauties – an early Express milk bottle, studded with instructions, and a vintage Co-Op one, rich in curlicue lettering. I was glad, though, that the young Joshua with the trumpet had gone. He wouldn't have understood.

Doing the Lambeth Walk

My passport to regular Lambeth walking was a Victorian silver watch. This machinery, weighty and of ample proportions, descended to me from my great-grandfather, who was on the editorial staff of a provincial Tory paper that earned itself the distinction of a mention by George Borrow. The watch, however, lacked a chain, and it seemed to me that the pawnbroker's in Lambeth Walk might provide one. There was no difficulty – they stocked Victorian watch chains – new ones – as if we were still in Imperial London, and other Victorian requisites, too, such as silver-mounted teething rings for infants. For 17s 6d I got a solid silver chain, complete with Albert, the whole thing being massive enough to anchor a Cunarder.

Having made my purchase, I found myself so fascinated by the market, the streets and the people that I stayed on for the rest of the day. It was a rich gâteau, composed of several layers – the lowest and thickest being the London of Mrs 'Arry 'Awkins and George Belcher and the topmost that of Vera Lynn. A subtle sprinkling of Herbert Morrison was the final touch, one that the finest chefs might include out. The smell of vegetables, fruit and pot plants mingled with the scent of Californian Poppy. Enchanting snatches of housewife's conversation insinuated themselves into one's ears. What you could get off points, the delusions of marriage, illness, death and anecdotes of budgerigars were the main topics.

Halfway down was the emporium of G. Body, Shirtmaker, hosier and hatter, wonderfully Keir Hardie or H. G. Wells. The windows were crammed with mufflers, union shirts and cloth caps (none of your sniffy exclusiveness of Bond Street or the Rue de la Paix). Inside were rows of green boxes, a yellow brown-grained counter and bentwood chairs with a pattern of holes for the ventilation of plebian behinds. Body's, to my regret, closed in 1969: the shop has been transmogrified into a jellied eel establishment. Opposite was a man who sold American funnies, startling pickles and various useless wartime gadgets, such as luminous buttons, reduced in price, for the war was over at last. I became a regular customer: I love Yankee comics.

My chief pleasure was in watching the pregnant or pram-pushing women go past the gravestones on display at the undertaker's – the alpha and omega of London life – diversified by the presence of careworn old men and women, who were, themselves, about to become the undertaker's customers.

A meal at the jellied eel shop or at Charley's opposite rounded off the treat. Charley's Dining Rooms remain with us, and Charley, still with his plants, real and plastic, in the windows, continues to offer Haddock, Kipper and Bloater Breakfasts. In those days, Lambeth Walk extended only up to where the Baths are now: the rest, up to the pub, was called China Walk. The old name can still be read on the wall of the Lambeth Walk, as the pub, originally plain Mason's Arms, has been called since 1951, when Lupino Lane did a public relations job on it.

The Walk has gone in for name dropping. It was originally Three Coney Walk, but the discovery of medicinal wells in the eighteenth century brought a temporary distinction to the district, and the street was unofficially rechristened Lambeth Walk as early as 1786. It appears in the rate books of 1811 for the first time under its present name. The wells and pleasure gardens have vanished; nevertheless, a fine late Georgian terrace still remains in Walnut Tree Walk to testify to the former quality of the neighbourhood.

Today, the wind of change, like the winds of autumn, blows through Lambeth Walk. The old thoroughfare – humble Cockney street, forum and agora in one – is on its way out: a G.L.C. shopping precinct will take its place. For the moment, enough survives among the rubble to make a connoisseur's sentimental journey worthwhile. One of these is the marine stores in Black Prince Road. 'You ought to come on Saturday,' said the owner, as I drew. 'We have the hippies an' swingers from over Chelsea way. They come for the old 1930 clothes, which they wear for their queer how d'ye dos. They only want long dresses, Palais-de-dance like. I tell you Saturday is the day for Lambeth Walk.'

St Andrew Undershaft

When I lived in Chelsea, I resolved always to visit a fresh church whenever I wanted to say my prayers and a new pub whenever I was thirsty, thus extending my knowledge of London as well as providing for spiritual and bodily needs. However, like all my gossamer resolutions, it had a short life: a fundamental dislike of change made me prefer the ones I already knew. Out of it, though, a sensible habit originated – that of visiting a given church several times during a month to study it in a leisurely fashion and thoroughly.

One I have recently been studying in this way is St Andrew Undershaft in St Mary Axe near the Baltic Exchange in the City. Most visitors will know it as the burial place of John Stow, historian and topographer of Pre-Fire London: his effigy is the subject of an annual ceremony, when a new quill pen is placed in the writer's hand by the Lord Mayor. But there is much more to the church than that. For one thing it is a virtually untouched survivor of medieval London, being undamaged in both the Great Fire and the Blitz: for another, it has rich treasures of stained glass, some of this being priceless heraldic Pre-Reformation glass now in store, awaiting a generous magnate or so to undertake the truly civilised task of putting it back into position. The church was re-built between 1520 and 1532, and it takes its curious name from the great maypole that once stood outside. Today giant office blocks tower about and round it, without, however, reducing it to insignificance: it holds its own among them like the chapel of an Oxford college somehow strayed among factories, quietly asserting the importance of old and beautiful things, a witness to the risen Christ alike to the faithful, the infidel and to those who couldn't care less. These old and beautiful things include the late Perpendicular nave arcade of six bays, the Harris organ, the pulpit and the East and West windows. The East window, a Crucifixion and Ascension with attendant saints and apostles, is a superb Victorian window of 1875 by Heaton Butler and Payne. It is almost good enough to be by Ford Madox Brown, though there is no mention of it in Hueffer's life of the artist. Anyhow, it is fine, and repays careful study: note the sunflowers characteristic of the period below the feet of the ascending Christ and the squared panes with olive leaves running behind the heads – all very typical of the motifs coined and issued by Morris and his associates.

What is now the West window, of brilliant rich colour, dates from 1637. Besides the royal arms, it shows five prominent Protestant sovereigns: Edward VI, Elizabeth, James I, Charles I and good King William of Orange. As the last was not on the throne when the window was made, he is obviously a replacement, very carefully matched in style and colour, for an earlier occupant of the light who can only be guessed: Charles II, the secret papist? But no guesswork is needed as to why the original monarch was tactfully banished, and if you look carefully when the sunlight strikes diagonally, slight differences in colour and texture can be detected. Below the King, the Dutch lion of the House of Orange is impaled on the English royal arms and, at the tip, William and Mary's initials are intertwined.

According to the notes for visitors, the tower was rebuilt in 1830, but this clearly relates only to the belfry stage and some of the quoins and the door: most of the masonry is certainly medieval. In all, St Andrew's is one of the City's most attractive ancient monuments and one that deserves its full share of care and attention, alike from casual visitors and city gents.

ST ANDREW UNDERSHAFT

Portrait of an Infantry Officer

'Knowing your mania for advertising bits and pieces,' said my young friend, Judith, one day, when I dropped in on her very personal junk shop, 'this might interest you. It's a new one on me.'

Whereupon she handed me a grey tin box. On the lid was a head and shoulders of a British officer of the old school – cap tilted rakishly, monocle and Sam Browne very dazzling, fresh complexioned, a wreath of smoke curling up from his cigarette – Captain Gingah, the nut with a cane, to the life. I said, 'Indeed it does interest me. In fact, I used myself to smoke his cigarettes. They were very good; I wish there were a few left in the tin to smoke while I tell you something worth knowing about him.'

Judith settled herself on a step ladder and I said, 'You have never seen an officer like him, nor have I. He packed up long ago, hopelessly outmoded, yet I am not sure that we are any the better off for his disappearance – not at all sure. He had no brains that anyone ever discovered – was fit for nothing, so it was said, but blanco and bullshit. His contempt for people like you and me was as boundless as his horizons were limited. He was perfectly ignorant about art – had never seen any beyond a regimental portrait. In a dim way he believed in the God of Battles, as long as they were British battles; in fact, he thought God was an Englishman. Had you pointed out that this could not be in the nature of things, he would have thought you a lunatic or a Bolshie, and would have demanded to know what else God could be, if not English? Whether he actually smoked Virginia cigarettes in the mess, I cannot say, since in those days anything but a Turkish cigarette was frowned upon by the officer class. And if you will turn to the *Iliad*, you'll find that one of its heroes was also partial to tobacco – I forget whether it was Ajax or Achilles – but he "spurs his steed, and smokes along the plain".'

'But,' said Judith, 'I could have told you all that more or less. Even 1950 vintage characters know it.'

'Have patience', I said, 'while I finish. Unbelievably, there was a man under that swaggering get-up, a man with a foolish heart ticking away under the military togs, one that was moved to indignation and pity when the Kaiser and his hordes moved in on the harmless Belgians and the gallant people of France. Of course, he was unaware that the common peoples of the world are very much alike – surprisingly so – that the great and everlasting division is not between them, but between ordinary Toms, Dicks and Harrys of whatever language or origin and all the leaders and authoritarians whatsoever or wheresoever. He didn't know that England was and still is as full of hateful Kaisers as

40

Prussia ever was, for, as I have told you, he wasn't a philosopher, wasn't with it. Neither are we, for that matter. We never ponder on history, never reflect on the undoubted fact that the vast miseries and evils that have afflicted mankind since the beginning have only rarely or occasionally been natural ones – famines, earthquakes and what not – but almost always those brought on by the unspeakable rascals who have impudently got power over us – the emperors, the governments and the shameless, degenerate ones amongst us who assist them. We never stop to think that there is no such thing as human authority – religious or secular – that no one has any right to make rules for us, that all such authority is an imposition and the pretence to it the most dangerous of fictions. Our friend with the fag wasn't up to that, Judith, didn't see that the English are beset by enemies among their own kind, as well as by those elsewhere. Didn't see that we must, somehow or another, rid ourselves once and for all of the politicians, the leaders, the haughty bureaucrats, the law and order men who have deluded and dis-ciplined us for centuries. Naturally, they perversely pretend that we voted for them or some of them, and all the interference with our liberties is for our own good – which is of course, the most ignoble sophistry conceivable. Our only redress, our only safety, is to rid ourselves of them, root and branch, and to make certain no others of the same ilk creep into the vacant places. I am not saying all is well with the common people: we are very lazy, increasingly greedy, heedless and restless, altogether distasteful; but we deserve better than to be disciplined from cradle to grave, don't you think?

'But I am forgetting about the man with the monocle. At least the Kaiser, the only enemy he could see, couldn't go on unchecked, whatever the final outcome. So he volunteered for the Front, along with a lot of others – pimply faced, pale complexioned bank clerks, grocers' assistants, all of them pawns of the generals and politicians, all of them fools: the bravest fools that were ever known, mediocrities of such a transcendent courage that even Death was awed at their passing.'

'And, of course,' mused Judith, 'your man got killed?'

'Very early on, when the fighting was still on open ground. But he was rubbed out a second time at Vimy, stopped a packet again on the Somme and finally, and worst of all, on the Marne.'

'He ought to have been more careful – having so many lives made him reckless.'

'That may be. But I had thought I'd lost sight of him, when one day I was looking through an exhibition of Great War photographs, enlarged from old negatives. And there he was, staring at me from the wall. No jaunty cap, of course, just a head on a pillow, but I recognised him at once. Never as long as I live shall I forget his eyes – the hopelessness of them. He had seen with them things that no man ought ever to look upon, and behind those things, always getting nearer, Armageddon itself. Another minute, and I've done. I told you you could see his eyes and the top of his head on the pillow. But nothing else. *Nothing else was there.* Bandages covered a fearful chasm; the upper and lower jaws, including the nose were clean gone – blown away by a shell with

Blighty written on it. He was being fed, in the few days that remained to him, on liquids. He wasn't even Captain Gingah any more – had become something larger, more universal, as it were. As he had no mouth, it was a case of no smoking. Not even Army Club.'

I bought the tin off Judith. As I left, I added, 'They used to have his portrait in Piccadilly before the last war, in electric lights. He was always puffing away up there, after dark – the portrait of an infantry officer, unknown by name or rank, deceased. But that was when Piccadilly was called the hub of the Empire, and we haven't got one any more.'

Waterloo Road

Waterloo Road, like most of South London, has not on the whole attracted much notice from the great ones of the earth. Once in a while, Royalty has lent a little fleeting light to its murky and unbecoming environs. Otherwise little attention has been accorded to it, and it remains downright unfashionable – a no man's land. Poets have failed to celebrate or apostrophise it; even the writers of music-hall songs who gathered at the now vanished York Hotel found in it nothing wherewith to furnish a ditty. The only exceptions to this neglect that I can think of are a few references by Dickens, a wartime film called *Waterloo Road* (a melodrama native to the Surrey side, only, of course, in battledress) and a large panorama, of which one sometimes sees prints, done at the turn of the century. The product of an artist who inscrutably called himself Lydia Dreams (the most unlikely pseudonym ever, apart from Sebastian Melmouth), this painting called 'Fame' has a foreground stuffed with music-hall stars of the day, constellated against a background formed by the railway bridge and St John's.

Yet Waterloo Road has its antiquities, though below ground. There are ancient Gothic arches and segmental windows buried at the East side of the traffic roundabout opposite the church: they were once in the garden of an early Victorian architect, L. N. Cottingham, who helped himself to various priceless souvenirs culled in the course of his restorations. When his house was demolished about 1961, the Gothic remains were simply walled up: I watched the workmen do it. Besides these are those of John of Gaunt's palace in the Strand, the stone from which, released by demolition at the time the Old Vic was built, was used to form foundations in the marshy soil: odd that 'time honoured Lancaster' should make an appearance on the stage above the remains of his old palace!

Still, it is the more recent scenery of the Waterloo Road that suits me best – the Lower Marsh market, one of the most interesting in South London and full of its peculiar character and vitality. Even if you have no use for bankrupt chemists' stock, transistors, plants, sexy books and hobnailed boots, you will surely appreciate the human element: and if not them, then the pre-Great War style shop of L. & N. Cohen, the House for Value, with clothes hung outside like the banners of Joshua's army, or the little house in Launcelot Street with its pavement garden flourishing in dustbins, boxes and old plastic buckets, with a lamp-post and gutter at the bottom instead of fairies.

Beyond David Grieg's shop (in what I term 'Montague Burton' or 'Selfridge' Classic) is, of course, the establishment of the tattoo artist 'Professor' Burchett at

No. 217 – now run by his son. This emporium has been written about many times, but its freshness and interest remains unimpaired, and a gaze into its crowded windows is worth a quarter of an hour of anyone's time. Besides offering a multiplicity of designs, sentimental, patriotic and oriental, including pictures of various full-bosomed belles from either the Barbary Coast or the naughty nineties or both, the concern announces that any design can be copied, crude work covered and that the treatment is painless and antiseptic.

Other pleasures lie in store. The Cut is dull today – its Victorian Saturday night vitality having utterly departed, but go down Greet Street for a view of small terraced houses with part of the Victorian Gothic St Andrew's School above the chimney stacks (a real Gothic nineteenth century school – precisely what schools ought to be like, if you must have them – I began my school days in just such a one, and loathed the instruction, despised the pedagogues, but fed on the building, and have never regretted it). This view is superbly framed by the railway arch.

Roupell Street (approach it by way of Windmill Walk, with the Kings Arms on one side and Phoebe's Florist's on the other, as I have drawn them, and the general stores opposite) is an astonishing example of latter-day London prosperity. Once it was a Street of dreary aspect, a place of love on the dole and pallid, none too particular kids. Now there are grey-painted doors, white window frames and brass knockers – the whole forming one of the trimmest streets out of Chelsea. I love it and its little shops on the corner, and visit it often with no small regret, for it is no more or less than a piece of Lancashire dropped somehow into London – the old Lancashire, I mean, of humble streets, bright hearths and cotton mills against a sunset sky of green and gold fading in the West – not the new one of cheap Spanish holidays and One Lung restaurants. Whittlesey Street and Theed Street behind are also worth seeing, though these are of larger, three-storied terraces, more in the usual London manner. Of course, the date, 1891, in a central pediment in Roupell Street is merely a later addition – the houses are earlier nineteenth-century industrial, like their above-mentioned northern counter-parts. A final pleasure, after the magic words 'Commit No Nuisance' twice repeated at the corner of Theed Street, is the old-fashioned sweet shop and newsagent's right at the corner of Roupell Street – grey, early nineteenth-century brickwork above, dark green painted woodwork below and a bit of nice lettering – precisely the kind of shop Whistler used to love to draw, and Walter Greaves too, in Chelsea, when the place was still a village, rents were low and swingers and trend setters a plague as yet unknown.

I don't know if you remember a periodical called *Passing Show*, price tuppence and full of ads for hair restorer, chest expanders and the Bennett ('Let Me Be Your Father') Correspondence College? Well, each week it had a coloured cover by that excellent artist in the Phil May tradition, Gilbert Wilkinson: the humours, always slightly far-fetched, were of London or its dolorous suburbs – a man in a gas mask carpet-beating and so on. I admired the skill of the drawings, whilst finding their subjects corny,

ROUPELL STREET AND WINDMILL WALK

unreal. But yesterday in Roupell Street I saw the thing in the flesh – ready for use, as it were – a small coloured boy stretching up to a copper offering him a lick at a whipped cream walnut. A pity, I thought, that *Passing Show* is defunct these many years, else I could have rung up the editor and sold him the idea, on the spot, for a bag of gold.

The Writing on the Wall

On the day that the Emperor of Abyssinia paid his quite properly delayed visit of reconciliation to Rome, I found myself, by pure chance, staring at the remains of an ancient slogan on a wall in one of the less exciting London suburbs. It said 'Mosley Speeks. Mosley Tonite.' On the instant, cohorts of blackshirted men marched up and down in the East End, bawling hideous anti-Jewish slogans from loose and ugly mouths. I found myself re-reading a crusty publication called *The British Italian Journal*, featuring alleged atrocity stories of the Abyssinian's cruelty to animals – as if the English themselves had never hunted a hapless creature to death or delivered one over to the vivisector's knife! Obviously this stale slogan still had life of a kind in it, a sort of twitching among bones, and I added it to my collection of mural messages.

This connoisseurship of painted walls, preferably faded, is a rewarding pastime, with the advantage that the collection so formed requires little storage space, no upkeep and no insurance. My own considerable collection began years ago when I used to be taken to Blackpool for holidays. The train approached that unique place on a long curve to the South Shore, and here one was treated to a view of the backsides of boarding houses. Each was painted on its gable with a huge and comforting message: 'Mrs Grundy from Wigan. Highly recommended', 'Mrs Platt from Farnworth. Good beds', 'Mrs Shuttleworth from Oldham. Home from Home'. These striking proclamations made a lasting impression: I began to look around for choice specimens, and there was no going back. I collect only permanent examples, amateur or professional. A collection of graffiti can be added, if you have a mind, though meaningless scrawls and moustaches from Underground posters are obviously unworthy of inclusion.

The practice of writing messages on walls is of ancient and honourable lineage. In Rembrandt's early composition, *Belshazzar's Feast*, of 1635 in the National Gallery, we see the turbaned monarch turning in peevish surprise to the discouraging message written in Hebrew on the wall, 'Weighed in the Balances and found wanting'. Obviously he is regretting his oversight in not appointing an experienced banqueting manager who would never have allowed such an untoward incident to take place. Between this and one that has recently appeared on a wall overlooking the railway at Vauxhall, advertising a current West End production (and next, incidentally, to a faded old one for George Grossmith at His Majesty's), there have been many messages. Some for Static Water Tanks can still be found – there is one on the Albert Embankment – and until recently there was the remains of a famous one on a wall near Aldgate, 'Open the Second Front Now'!

The gem of my own collection was gathered a year or two ago in Central London: I would not part with it for all the Old Masters at Sotheby's. It reads 'Keep Billy Graham off the Moon'. No sentence in the English language can compare with it, so utterly mad is it in all its parts, except perhaps William Blake's 'Caterpillar upon the leaf repeats to thee thy Mother's grief', and even this has a wild logic absent from the other.

Adverts for commercial products, especially if defunct, are desirable items: an example of this remains on the wall of a Waterloo Road cafe, 'The Sunday Referee. Most enterprising paper of the Age'. Also collectors' pieces are those for soaps, early cinemas and working men's hostels, particularly if displaying a pointing hand and a bit of sleeve. Only last week I acquired a new specimen, previously uncatalogued. This, a sprayed message, came from the Euston Road (why are these murals always sprayed nowadays – is the good old brush lettering on its way out?), and it asserted that 'The tigers of wrath are wiser than the horses of instruction' – a message that seems for a moment profound and is then seen to be totally devoid of meaning.

Back then to the old brush lettering, however much it trickled! Back to terseness, instant comprehension! Mosley Tonite!

If London wall writings are not enough to satisfy the appetite that grows with the feeding, there are country ones to form a further collection, like this one culled from a brick wall in Horsham:

Denne Road
Livery and Bait Stables

Brakes for Picnic Parties

Open and Closed
Rubber Tyred Carriages
For Hire

A mute reminder of the days that are no more, when picture hats and serge skirts were the thing, along with alpaca jackets and straw boaters, when affairs – in spite of what sentimentalists have claimed to the contrary – went well, went very well indeed.

Out of my own country bunch, the prize bloom, surpassing all others for magnificence, is one sent to me by a generous professor at Liverpool University. Found by him on a wall in the Midlands, it is, like Keats's urn, a joy for ever. It reads

Vote Tory
The Kingdom of Bevan is Nye.

TOBACCO SHOP WALL, RATHBONE PLACE

Marylebone Revisited

Until recently a weather-stained board outside Marylebone Station advised the public that 'Coaches for Athens start here'. It is not, however, necessary to venture so far afield to study the architectural remains of a vanished civilisation: those of the English can be conveniently studied in the area between the station and Edgware Road, and the artifacts of that ancient people – china models of Blackpool Tower, jerries, faded photographs, old gas fires, plastic gnomes and copies of *Chatterbox* – can be contemplated by the antiquarian on the junk stalls of the quarter, notably in Church Street on Saturday.

The station itself is a relic of a departed age. Generally the facade – excepting the magnificent glass and iron portico linking the station to the former hotel – has the look of a late and great Victorian country house. Even today in mid-afternoon, the Victorian atmosphere is still strong, reminding me nostalgically of arriving at Southport in earlier days, with the whole of Lord Street to look forward to and a military band playing under the trees of that choice thoroughfare. As a grim prototype of the shape of things to come, Edgware Road, on the far side of this area, is sinister and depressing beyond belief. The new cop shop towers menacingly over what is left of the old terraces and shops: there are vast and meaningless blocks of flats, the whole making the old remains appear a crumbling anachronism. What is so macabre is that the background has changed, but the people have not. Only yesterday I met an old woman wrapped in layers of shawls, pushing a strange contraption and accompanied by her two dogs on strings, the humble trio being as unlike the brave new Edgware Road as possible. Farther along the concrete jungle, an ancient, cloth-capped patriarch was selling pencils ('made in the Republic of China') and exercise books. No one was patronising him, and so I moved in, particularly as I have a fondness for cheap exercise books with multiplication tables on the backs. I found their Edwardian art nouveau covers had been overprinted with decimal conversion tables – an act of purest vandalism – and pointed out to the old man that he in selling and I in buying them were both of us taking part, albeit minute, in a colossal bamboozle. He turned his watery eyes on me, and said he knew it. He knew dezzimals was what nobody wanted, nohow, but that there was nothing we could do about it, for *they* (and I wish I could convey the emphasis he put into the pronoun) will allus screw us in the end. I was so depressed that I took myself off for a quarter of an hour's gaze in the windows of the wonderful old-fashioned drapers in Bell Street, where they still sell woollen interlock pants and singlets and twill aprons for boys, to

LISSON GROVE COTTAGES, MARYLEBONE

recover. Still, even there, the horror of the innovations pursued me, for I thought, 'What boys wear twill aprons (as they did outside Victorian grocers in old photographs) in the appalling decimal age, at once concrete and discrete?' The times are out of joint and interlock underpants with them!

Flats and shops are now going up on the site of the Royal West London, home of melodramas starring sagacious dogs, until recently another of the classic ruins, for only the Tuscan portico remained. These flats cover the site, on Penfold Street, of the old flea market, a place in which to buy advertising ashtrays, old telephones and books of sermons – everything, in fact, that no one wanted – cheap off the pavement. Even the men's lavatory in Church Street has gone in for stainless steel, trendy mosaic walls and push-button drying equipment. How I regret the loss of the tiles, the gleaming copper and brass, the old enamelled warnings against VD! Fortunately, half of the street – the better half, junk-wise – is still intact. The catalogue of finds I have collected here reads like the visiting list of a demented jackdaw: a water colour by Martin Hardie, a glass dish, advertising Swiss milk chocolate, from a sweet shop, various toys, pottery and, most recently, a collection of cards of working men's buttons ('The Briton Card of Buttons. Strong and Durable').

Round the corner is Lisson Grove Post Office, a survival of the old village life of the district. By its side is a narrow passage which leads to a backwater not to be missed. In it are the Lisson Grove Cottages, in style Industrial Revolution combined with Peabody, where the small, egg-box gardens are covered with netting to discourage nocturnal visits by the neighbourhood's cats. The whole is an untouched survival of old Marylebone: see it next time you visit the post office to draw your old-age pension.

Commercial Gothic

For whatever reason, examples of the Gothic Revival are scarce in the City, apart from a few churches – and these early – and this is the more remarkable in view of the fact that so much of the 'square mile' was rebuilt during the ascendancy or hegemony of Victorian Gothic. Elsewhere, especially in the industrial North, the romantic ideals of the Revivalists spread to a degree quite astonishing, until one reflects that the Lancashire industrialists were among the very earliest supporters of the Pre-Raphaelites, but the commercial hierarchy of the City remained more or less aloof from the fervour outside, most likely from an innate conservatism that persisted until very recently. Queen Victoria Street has a number of office blocks that can be classed as Gothic if only because they cannot be described as anything else, but it is poor stuff, merely run up in response to a fashion; there were one or two Gothic warehouses (one by William Burges) in Thames Street – all now demolished, which leaves but three outstanding examples. These are the former Bank of Australasia in Lothbury (Ruskinian: a marble Venetian palace and quite splendid) and the two I illustrate – Suffolk House at the bottom of Laurence Pountney Hill and the Gothic office in Eastcheap. Suffolk House has now gone: I include it among the memorials of things that were. Or rather, there is a new Suffolk House on the site – a glass hive entirely out of harmony with the mellow, eighteenth century rectory and merchants' houses adjoining (which the Victorian Suffolk House never was) and with the dreariest fountain that the mind of man can conceive at the rear, one that more accurately resembles a leaking silage container than anything the word 'fountain' ought to conjure up. It is true that Suffolk House was not Victorian Gothic at its most significant: there was nothing intriguing, original or memorable about it: it could not compete with parallel examples in Manchester or Liverpool, and its detailing left much to be desired. Yet I never saw it without a thrill of recognition – the recognition that, despite its being a commercial job for commercial ends, a genuine infusion of a romantic ardour had somehow taken place. The building had vitality and an appeal not easily analysed, like that of a mongrel dog, and as hard to gainsay, in contrast to Victorian Gothic of a more respectable pedigree – eminently that of Scott, which leaves us uninterested, unmoved and empty-handed at the end of the day. That the City is the poorer for its disappearance is beyond doubt.

Fortunately, a happier fate seems in store for the Gothic office building in Eastcheap, designed by R. L. Roumieu, normally a purveyor of restless Gothic of doubtful provenance. It was built as the London depot of Hill, Evans and Company, British

Geoff Fletcher 1968

Suffolk House
Laurence Pountney
Hill

SUFFOLK HOUSE

GOTHIC OFFICES, EASTCHEAP

wine and vinegar manufacturers, and had originally a centre pedimented door on the ground floor, flanked by a pair of openings composed of door and window on each side. All this lower part of the facade has now gone, except for the door on the left or western side. Above this the facade remains in statu quo, a fascinating affair in which movement manages to stop short of restlessness or even feverishness, though by only a few degrees. When 'The Builder' illustrated this unique example of the high Victorian Gothic office on October 10th, 1868, the journal described the style as 'Gothic of the South of France with a Venetian impress', adding judiciously that 'the design, if a little overdone, may be considered picturesque and original'. Picturesque and original is, I think, a fair comment, though the originality is, of course, not that of an artist of Butterfield's calibre, in which the historic elements have been melted down and re-issued with the designer's image and superscription stamped upon them. It consists largely in a certain audacious ingenuity in the assembling of parts. In a word, Butterfield made everything he borrowed his own, which is what a great artist always does, as Wilde remarked in one of the more truthful of his half-truths, and, lacking this authority, Roumieu's design lacks a corresponding integrity.

Still, it is all great fun, and fun is an ingredient now entirely lost to architecture. We shall never more build sham ruins nor blow delectable Indian bubbles at seaside watering places. We build not for commodotie, firmnesse or delight, but only to house computers. The most striking feature of the elevation is the range of deeply recessed windows, casting Victorian shadows, an effect aided by the six projecting canopied niches, which cast long diagonal shadows; these, coming and going, give a feeling of movement to the facade. Slender shafts, standing out against these darks, give a strong vertical accent, and the intersecting of mouldings is arranged with an adroitness and stylishness that must have seemed very novel and modish at the time. French influence is paramount, the 'Venetian impress', as far as I can see, amounting to no more than the circular disks surrounded by the familiar Venetian alternate billet moulding, which is repeated on the large upper arches. Roumieu's instinct in this design (unless it was a lesson learned from Butterfield) was to avoid much decorative sculpture and place the charming roundel of the head of a fox peering through grasses at the most telling point – at the centre – where it forms the crowning feature of a two light, sharply pointed, lancet window, truncated in the heads. The sculpture is by Frampton and Williamson.

Of course, the total effect is grievously marred by the crude and unfeeling way in which the modern shops have been jammed in below, in a sort of shot-gun marriage, destroying proportions and balance. Curious and eccentric though it may be, the former vinegar depot reflects back, as from an imprisoned mirror, the astonishing vitality of the splendid decade that found its architectural expression in the High Victorian Gothic style, and hid its misgivings in the shadow of an equilateral pointed arch.

Bloomsbury:
Datur Hora Quieti

Each year in the week before Christmas, I indulge myself in a grand tour of Bloomsbury, always in accordance with an unvarying established routine worthy as to its
changelessness with my unenterprising Chinese ancestors. Each year I find myself
deploring, as Charles Lamb might, the innovations that have afflicted 'those good old
Tory brick-built streets' or even finding parts of it unrecognisable: I am overtaken by
new men and new architecture, like Rip Van Winkle. Why I refer my sentimental
journey to the Christmas season, I cannot logically account for, except that Marchmont
Street, now generally so reduced in interest, takes on at that season something dis-
tantly resembling its former attraction as a shopping street and a scruple or two of its
old vitality and character.

Christmas in Bloomsbury is signalled for me by the appearance of snow men,
puddings and Christmas cakes in the ABC on the Euston Road, where in that charming
combination of catering and Dickens, I launch my tour. This is the foundation: the
corner stone is always tea in my old favourite corner cafe, where the aspidistras, mind-
ful of the Biblical injunction, have been fruitful and have multiplied down the years so
that the place bids fair to rival the Palm House at Kew in the matter of vegetation.
Underneath the glossy green banners of the plants gather for refreshments certain
ancient inhabitants, survivors from some long discredited Labour Government. They
bear the accounts of each other's ailments and afflictions with a wonderful sympathy,
whilst the hot water geyser issues its clouds of ascending steam, and the proprietor, by
means of a festive card (itself a hardy perennial), offers season's greetings to all his
customers.

Between these two events – as West End drapers occasionally term their sales – I
fit in a number of time-honoured observances, such as mooning in Woburn Walk – in
these days much more sprightly than when I was a student – and Burton Street nearby,
more or less *status quo ante*, but for the disappearance of dead-end kids – a street likely
to attract the attentions of developers sooner or later. I treat myself to a long and loving
stare in the windows of the Home and Colonial in Marchmont Street. How greatly I
admire that title 'Home and Colonial' and the strength of mind that retains it nowadays:
I really must do some research on these multiple grocers and find out why so many –
Liptons, The Meadow, The Maypole and the rest, including defunct ones like the

Queen's Tea Company – suddenly sprang up in gold and plate glass and marble in the nineties.

I view the Christmas tree in Russell Square, always fine, or those in the yard of the Children's Hospital and that on the entrance to Corams Fields – a touch that the large-hearted, good Captain would endorse; or I visit Dickens's house with its spanking, beribboned wreath on the door: he, too, would approve of that, no one more so.

But this year I made a fatal error. I began the wrong way round, and got myself in what was Woburn Square before London University made it the horror it has become. The sight of bearded, dark-spectacled or long-skirted students, mostly looking as if tailored by a rag merchant and pushing infants in prams, ought to have warned me off. But I wanted to see Christ Church, built by Vulliamy in 1830, one of the several examples of that London curiosity, the Gothic church built to serve the religious life of an otherwise classical square – the lamb lying down with the lion. I wanted to spend an hour or so in it, because it is now likely to be declared redundant. I, myself, think that a church can never be redundant. If of no merit architecturally, it is at least a witness for Christ, which is more than can be said of many of the clergy – the priests of Rome on the one hand, deceitful pedlars of vain superstition like those older pretenders, the priests of ancient Egypt, or the clerics of the Established Church, servile for the most part before the hateful secular authoritarians, the whole mass of them absurdly taking upon themselves the right to instruct us.

Now that my temper has cooled off somewhat, I can admire the church, or, rather, its exterior, for its internal arrangements are merely those of a preaching house, being designed before the scientific study of Gothic churches had got under way – before the ecclesiologists had discovered and prescribed fit and proper rules and before such architectural misdeeds as the use of cast iron ornament (there is much of it – well but coldly designed at the entrance to Christ Church under the tower) had been declared scandalous – in brief, in the pre-Pugin era. The tower and spire of Christ Church are far too good to lose – the former with its deeply recessed ogee arches and panelling and the latter with cunningly arranged buttresses and offsets, combining with the parapet to form a motif striking and original throughout its entire length, including the entrance below – a state of affairs often achieved by the early Gothicists before too great a dependence on medieval prototypes put an end to the free handling of Gothic elements for a couple of decades.

Beyond this there is one consideration that makes the idea of destroying Christ Church so shocking, for it was there that the gifted, gentle, melancholy Christina Rossetti worshipped when she lived, out of the great world and the lights of her brilliant brother, in Torrington Square. What depths of imbecility and degradation have we not sunk to when we can contemplate destroying a building sanctified by her?

I stood in the porch meditating over this, thinking of her under the grass of the great and terrible North London cemetery, watching the workmen on the new and

CHRIST CHURCH, WOBURN SQUARE

horrible buildings of that once demure square and listening to the scratch of the plane leaves as the wind blew them about the pavements this way and that as the December day gave in to mist and murky twilight. Not for the first time I wondered what the hell it was all about:

> . . . . Hearken what the past doth witness and say:
> Rust in thy gold, a moth is in thine array,
> A canker is in thy bud, thy leaf must decay.
> At midnight, at cockrow at morning, one certain day
> Lo, The Bridegroom shall come and shall not delay:
> Watch thou and pray.
> Then I answered: Yea.

A Dealer in Magic and Spells

Whereas the British Museum specialises in antiquities, Davenport's, immediately opposite its main entrance, specialises in novelties – or rather in novelties, jokes and puzzles for young people and in supplying illusions to professional and amateur magicians. A constant stream of visitors of all ages (Prince Charles has recently been among them) penetrates into the shop's dusty interior, from the small boy anxious to acquire a new set of vampire teeth to serious magicians seeking new and impressive tricks to mystify their audiences.

The business was founded in 1898 by Lewis Davenport, a music hall conjuror, and is now run by his granddaughter, Miss Betty Davenport. The founder's photograph hangs on the wall behind the counter, along with one of his friend, Houdini. Curiously enough, both got themselves involved with Spiritualism, for Lewis Davenport was often called in by the police to sniff out the methods used by crooked mediums in the old days of table turning seances, and Houdini, later in life, made a special study of the exposure of ghostly humbug and spiritual spoof.

I told Miss Davenport that such feats as the Floating Lady and sawing through a woman had always fascinated me since as a small boy I saw Horace Goldin perform the allegedly impossible Indian Rope trick. I asked her if she thought that unhandy persons such as myself could learn to saw through a woman. After eyeing me critically for a time, she replied yes, but it was inadvisable and that she preferred not to enlighten me on the whole. The firm has a warehouse in which is kept a large stock of old illusions. 'When magicians retire', Miss Davenport told me, 'we buy up their illusions.' Now, surely that is the greatest novelty of all, this selling of one's illusions, my own usually being shattered by other people, or else I just lose them, long before I get round to selling them. But there is more to the shop than this. What makes it so unique and so attractive to those with children to entertain or Christmas stockings to fill is the unbelievable number of Edwardian novelties that one can still obtain here, for Davenport's have been in existence for so long that old stocks, tucked away in cardboard boxes, are still being found. Small toys and novelties that were made in pre-1914 Germany to be sold for a penny or so can be bought either by the nostalgically minded or by those who want to give today's children a rare treat from the day before yesterday. There are hundreds of matchbox toys, either with little sets of building bricks inside or else a tiny model of a farm or a fire brigade at work. Then there are old (but new) conjuring outfits 'made in Bavaria', Victorian pocket watches that explode with a bang when opened, comic and fortune-telling postcards that people sent before the Kaiser rolled up the map of Europe and vintage puzzles: Davenport's can find you almost anything, given time. Patrick Page, their magician manager, is expert at dis-interring these pleasures of past times, and he produced for me a big box of that most delightful of Victorian paper toys, the flicker-graph, humble provider of living pictures before Hollywood or TV was ever heard of. Some small boys watched me as I flicked over the little booklets, bringing Pierrot and Clown into jerky Edwardian life. One said he supposed I used to play with such things before motion pictures came in. As they 'came in' in the 1890s, I was somewhat taken aback, but I said nothing, for to be dis-illusioned in a shop devoted to illusions is the last thing anybody wants.

They have even had visits from African witch doctors anxious to possess them-selves of the white man's magic, wherewith to bamboozle the innocents at home with anything except, I suppose, black face soap. It was from Africa that Davenport's received a touching letter containing a request that even they could not grant: a native girl, having lost a great toe, wrote to them for a magic potion – an uncanny spell – or whatever occult thing they could provide to make a new toe appear in place of the old. Sadly, the powerful Davenport ju-ju was not up to that one, even though they can conjure up out of dusty cardboard boxes a fair number of other human bits and pieces – chattering teeth, wobbly hands, skulls and false noses, for instance.

DAVENPORT'S MAGIC SHOP

With a Nice Girl in the Park

I forget whether the advice to study large maps was Melbourne's or Palmerston's, but if you take it and look at a large one of London, you will be astonished at the amount of public parkland and open spaces – all for your pleasure. Some are small like the David Copperfield Garden in New Kent Road and the Bethnal Green Gardens or that delightful one with Tudor-style teahouse at the foot of Putney Bridge. Some like Kenwood and Holland Park were once the grounds of private residences, others are Royal Parks. Many of the most surprising and rewarding were created by the Victorians, and are well worth the visitor's attention as a change from the more celebrated breathing spaces.

By a coincidence, a reader has just sent me an interesting collection of old postcards of Southwark Park. They were photographs taken a thousand years ago in the reign of King Edward VII, when people liked to listen to the soldiers in the Park and admire the bedding-out plants or take a boat on the lake on a Sunday afternoon. At least that is what they are doing on the postcards, all dressed up in serge skirts, button boots and straw boaters, and they were wiser than they knew. With a nice girl in the Park!

I used to live near Southwark Park myself once, and can recommend it: there is a charming and well stocked lake, a rose garden, an open air swimming pool and a restaurant, all as unlike the neighbouring Jamaica Road as could be.

Battersea Park is the largest one in the old County of London, south of the Thames. Very nearly two hundred acres in extent, it was laid out by Nash's pupil, Sir James Pennethorne, and opened by Queen Victoria in 1858. Its regular features include the sixteen-acre lake, the Old English Flower Garden and the fallow deer in their own enclosure. But there is much more to it than this. There is the Children's Zoo, opening at Easter and containing a variety of friendly animals from guinea pigs to pigmy donkeys and some notable parrots, toucans and other wise birds (the nominal charge also covers admission to the Fairground), a children's boating lake, a club for under five year olds and various playgrounds. Besides this, Battersea Park is the setting for such entertainments as the Easter Parade and the Royal Tournament March Past and the light orchestral, jazz and folk concerts at the Concert Pavilion on the north carriage drive.

Farther afield is the park of the Crystal Palace on Sydenham Hill. The Palace was destroyed by fire in 1936, and the grounds lay largely derelict after the last war. But now the seventy-acre park has taken on a new lease of life, and the improvements include a

THE LAKE, SOUTHWARK PARK

rock and water garden and a new restaurant. Its main attractions are still the prehistoric monsters left by the Victorians, the boating and the fishing lake and the children's zoo and play park and, for the adults, the open-air concerts, motor and motor cycle racing.

Lastly, two more out of a long list to tempt you to experiment – the Cutty Sark Gardens at Greenwich and Geffrye's Garden in Shoreditch. The first part of the Cutty Sark Gardens was opened in 1957, and the most recent extension in 1967, each side of the old dock gates. There are plans for the future development of the area. Meantime, apart from the Cutty Sark and the Gipsy Moth IV, there is here a perfect vantage point for the ever-changing river scenes, and pop concerts, band concerts and children's shows are staged in the summertime.

The Geffrye's Garden was opened as a park in 1912, when the almshouses were converted into what is now one of the most delightful museums in London, for youngsters as well as grown-ups, and in the park are a playground and a netball court and various shows are given for children in the summer.

In all, my advice is to sample some of them, even if you haven't got button boots, a serge skirt or a celluloid collar; in fact, it might be advisable *not* to wear any of these. When I recently revisited Southwark Park, the only ancient landmarks from the picture postcard I could find were the cast iron gas lamps, fortunately still surviving on its fine, sweeping 'inner ring'. Gone, too, were the dead-end kids – not of the Edwardian age merely, but those of my much more recent period of residence. In their place were up-to-the-minute mothers, bouncing with National Health, kids likewise, togged up to the nines, feeding the ducks and accompanied by well groomed dogs – Alsatians, collies, golden retrievers. The shabby, pathetic, down-at-paw pariahs of Rotherhithe, lean in the rib cage and woebegone in manner, that in days of yore gave one so much to be depressed about, have been replaced by a happier breed. In such circumstances, I think an Eton collar and ill-fitting boots might seem out of place after all.

The Simpler Pleasures of London

When I first visited London as a schoolboy in 1934 I had two things marked on my official programme – to see the capital *en fête* for the wedding of Princess Marina and to devote time to seeing the great sights. What I actually did was to carry out a private scheme which consisted of hanging about the precincts of Broadcasting House in the hope of seeing Henry Hall. I don't regret this – in fact I would do it again tomorrow, if Henry would only show up – but it launched me on a career of never seeing the things everyone else does, or rarely. However, I take consolation from the undoubted truth in Mark Twain's remark that our eagerness to see celebrated things is easily accounted for: it is not because of what we ourselves see in them that our enthusiasm is kindled, but because of what *others* have seen in them; nearly all our wonder is secondhand.

Still, recently it has seemed to me time to take a short holiday from funeral parlours, flyblown caffs, betting shops – all my customary delights – and sample once again the simpler pleasures not enough indulged in, and also to catch up on those so obvious that I have never done them at all. Therefore, I have been to the waxworks, idled in the parks, climbed the Monument, visited the Abbey and St Paul's and fed the pigeons in Trafalgar Square. I have even been to the zoo. Not that I really care for zoos. The prospect of captive animals on exhibition for the benefit of humans fills me with shame. Besides, there is something unutterably sad about many of them – elephants and bison, for instance – so that it is difficult to decide which lowers one's spirits more – the inmates or the visitors. Nonetheless, the Zoological Gardens, as the Victorians would call them, are exceptionally well contrived and run, and there are always children fraternising with the animals in the way Providence intended them to, which cheers one up.

But I liked the Monument. I liked the man in the Monument, too, who sat on a wooden chair, a High Priest in shirt sleeves. I liked the way he chuckled when one of the two children I had with me complained that you couldn't see the Fire, and I had to explain that it had been put out some time before our visit. The view from the abacus of the column is certainly worth the climb, when once you have overcome the conviction that the whole thing is about to fold in on itself and topple. It is even worth the ludicrous two and a half new pence you pay instead of the honest tanner. And, of course, we went to the Horse Guards, where my young friends made other diverting, fresh-minted remarks, causing the sentry, catching my eye, to close his in a prodigious wink, a wink that had done good service on other notable occasions – such as Waterloo and Sebastopol.

I am not sure about the new glass doors to St Paul's – they appear to have escaped from a prestige office block – but I did enjoy the monuments, which nobody else does. I love draperies, tassels, laurel wreaths and weeping Britannias carried out realistically in marble, though I know I shouldn't. I am not sure about the waxworks, either, much as I love murders. They are too skilful, too lifelike, too close to real human beings to be quite comfortable. I think on the whole I prefer a travelling waxworks, *à la* Mrs Jarley, I once saw, in which the ancient, knocked-about statesmen had not only changed their jobs as adroitly as in real life, but also their names; by the addition of a pipe and bowler, Philip Snowden had become Stanley Baldwin, and Dr Crippen, less moustache but plus brown boot polish, was transmogrified into Dr Ruxton.

On the whole, it was lounging in Regents Park that I liked best – a return to an old, disused custom of mine. It was good to lounge in a deckchair on the daisy-spangled grass and listen to the honking of the Chinese geese, thinking of nothing in particular and dreamily eyeing the boats on the water. It was better still to take lunch in the open air at the Rose Garden Restaurant. I had no sooner started to eat when a company of sparrows arrived to perch hopefully on the edge of the table, and a brown and grey pigeon, unusually bold, came to sit on my plate. How nice it was to feel his warm, soft breast against my hand as we both stowed away the food, while the sparrows cocked their beady eyes! Of course, you can guess the outcome. I was made to feel a perfect heel by those birds, and so gave up my lunch to them altogether – which is what they had intended all along – and let them wade in, while I sat back and smoked.

Animals and birds have always got the upper hand of me this way, very early in the acquaintance. They quickly divine the sincere respect I have for their superior qualities. They see that I am soft-centred where they are concerned, and once possessed of this knowledge, the game is up. In my Gloucester Place days, when the London evenings in the summer were hot and airless, I got to rowing on the lake, mainly to visit a water rat. He had a comfortable little dug-out on a banking, and sat at the entrance most evenings, washing his ears and thinking about this and that – about *The Wind in the Willows* perhaps. He was quite tame, and as befits a Cockney gentleman, little given to nervousness. If you rested your oars he would quietly proceed with his toilet until, having had enough of it and you, he vanished with a flick of the tail.

Otherwise, my most satisfactory moments in Regents Park were the times when I went to admire the display of tulips presented by the people of my beloved Holland, accompanied by my Cairn, whose job it was to superintend the business of feeding the ducks and pigeons with sliced bread; the whole being rounded off by supper at The Volunteer, where animals of all sorts were welcome, for the proprietor was the last of the magnificent London public house landladies. Most of her customers had been going there for decades – long enough, in fact, to be accepted as equals by The Volunteer's

REGENTS PARK

parrots, who picked up bits of pie crust below decks, in between bouts of chaffing the regulars and calling for pints of bitter. It was a notable hostelry, The Volunteer.

I have been looking again at those scenes in Southwark Park, taken before the Great War. Now, I used myself to take a turn there when I lived in Bermondsey, when the hot pavements and close-smelling streets indicated a session on the grass and a sniff at the roses that bloomed in its lowly air; but it is plain that that the park was nothing then to what it had been in Edwardian summers. One postcard shows them pulling manfully on the oars, their heads shaded by billycocks or boaters. On another, Bermondsey kids – got up for the occasion in knickerbockers and pinafores (always pinafores over serge skirts) – are sitting on benches. It was a curious thing, come to think of it, to mark the Sabbath by donning a suit kept for the purpose. What difference could it make to God whether they were genteel or shabby, clean or unwashed? Clearly they were simpletons, ripe for the harvest the politicians were preparing, ready for the threshing floor. But now that Londoners have put aside worsted stockings and aprons in favour of hot pants and skin divers' watches and are no longer ignorant – now that their pleasures are complicated instead of simple – are they much the happier for it?

'Is there – is there balm in Gilead?
Tell me – tell me, I implore!'
Quoth the Raven, 'Nevermore'

Meditations in Billingsgate

No London thoroughfare has changed so much in character or lost so much in interest as Thames Street, Upper and Lower, from The Mermaid to the Tower. Warehouses, classic and gothic, old pubs and ancient, dark and mysterious riverside alleyways have come under the hammer. In their place have come erections of a relentless dullness and mediocrity with no more of architectural qualities about them than may be obtained from a child's box of wooden bricks and considerably less interest to boot. The Billingsgate area has suffered a decline of atmosphere along with the rest of the area, for apart from losses such as the Coal Exchange (a vandalistic demotion that nothing can ever put right), there has been a loss of character caused by the intrusion, without regard to effect, of contemporary blocks totally incompatible with the traditional, authentic character of the area.

Lovat Lane is a typical example; nothing has been destroyed but its quality, and this solely as a result of a glass office block towering over its old skyline, as seen from Billingsgate, with the result that the old view uphill past the Iron Warehouse and St Mary at Hill has no pleasure left in it. One is now confined to a down-hill view or giving the whole thing up. Nonetheless, I still like to moon around there, savouring what is left of its former atmosphere and loitering in those few alleys still intact and unspoiled by mindless interpolations, as Botolph Alley, for instance. Here is nothing for the architect of the new age but everything for the lovers of what was once the City of London's great feature – the combination of parish church and network of narrow alleys. There is Beazley's, the tea and coffee merchants, who used to have an old-fashioned Staffordshire tea pot in the window, comforting and inviting to the customer. They still display saucers full of exotic teas, like jasmine flower and the wonderfully named gunpowder. There are two old-fashioned cafés good to behold and as far removed from the fast moving steak houses and neon lit foodoramas as may be: the one in my drawing, painted Brunswick Green, with the remains of a hanging gas lamp, and George's opposite, with sausages, steaks and jam roll steaming in the window – and custard too – all hot. The grey brick embattled tower of St Mary at Hill (built in 1780 to replace the decayed pre-Fire tower left by Wren in his rebuilding) is too austere to give any hint of the extremely beautiful church that lies behind. St Mary's is worth an hour's quiet study on several accounts. The interior as it now appears after several modifications is quite one of the most perfect in the City – the high watermark of Protestantism as applied to the creation of a parish church – Protestantism as a positive thing, that is, not merely the innocuous residuum after the revolting lies and superstition have been sieved out. The church is so peaceful that one might be miles away in a deep countryside instead of Billingsgate, which you spell with four letters, on the doorstep. You can hear the blackbirds sing in the plane trees of the charming alley by the side of the church. Everything here is to be savoured slowly – the delicate Adam-style ceiling put up in the late 1840s by that most admirable architect, James Savage, the fine old pews, the Baroque altar and splendid carved pulpit with a great sounding board, the wrought iron sword rests and the carvings – grapes, pineapple, pine cones, oak leaves and musical instruments – on the front panels of the organ gallery. St Mary's is a model church in respect of maintenance, too; nothing could exceed the loving care that so obviously goes into its preservation. Here are held the services in thanksgiving for the harvest of the sea: a curious proceeding, I always think, in Billingsgate or where-ever men go down to the sea in ships, for it seems odd to me to bring about the deaths of thousands of God's creatures of the finny tribe and then to offer thanks to Him for delivering them into our hands. It may not seem so as you eat your morning kipper or supper-time oyster: it only comes home in its horror when you see piles of helpless crabs, alive but doomed, in the markets of Venice, trout kept in tanks in the restaurants of London and Paris and eels cut up alive on the London stalls. You then realise that the prayer should be one of forgiveness, not of thanksgiving, and that it is better to avoid either and to leave these creatures of the sea – from shrimps to whales – in the place where they belong, to enjoy the short slice of eternity to which they have a right. The cats of the area, however, have no such scruples, and you will find them, when the main business of the day is over, quietly despatching some fishy morsel, and even the blackbirds are not above pecking at the odd winkles that hang around the old cobbles of Lovat Lane.

You can rest after your wanderings in the churchyard garden of St Dunstan in the East. The making of this was an imaginative act, and so was the part restoration of the church walls and tracery. Where on earth the masons who are skilled enough to copy the old mouldings were obtained from I do not know, but they were old time crafts-men, and, as I watched them at work, I wondered how I, if a practising architect, would set about the task of finding them. Wren lived in Idol Lane nearby for a time during the building of St Paul's – actually lived there, which he never did in the old house on Bankside that claims this distinction – and the tower and spire of St Dunstan's, one of his best Gothic essays, was one in which he took a certain pride. Fortunately it escaped damage when the church, a nineteenth-century rebuilding of no particular merit, was gutted by war-time bombing. One or two old trees on the south side of the church were sacrificed in the making of the garden. One regrets this, while being compelled to admire the skill and care that has gone into the new layout, a care that even extends to the erection of two fine early nineteenth-century bollards of cast iron, painted black so they resemble succulent sticks of liquorice, set at the rear opposite the offices of Gill and Duffus.

BOTOLPH ALLEY, BILLINGSGATE

Brooke's Market
Geoffrey Fletcher 1972

BROOKE'S MARKET, HOLBORN

Uncommon Market

Brooke's Market is the most dry as dust, out of the way, corner in a hole in all central London. A market where nothing is sold, Brooke's has wooden seats on which hardly anyone ever sits and a fountain no one ever drinks from: nobody ever seems to go there with any distinct purpose, except as a bird of passage, going somewhere else. Unlike certain other markets – Shepherd Market or the so-called Caledonian – it is entirely unfashionable. It takes its name from Fulke Greville, Lord Brooke, a friend of Sir Philip Sidney. It was in Brooke House in September, 1628, that Lord Brooke was stabbed to death by a vengeful valet – a gentleman's un-gentleman who discovered he was missing from the beneficiaries of his lordship's will. Nonetheless, ignoring the facts, I like to think that Brooke was a Victorian landlord, with heavy jowl and side-whiskers, rack-renting in what was then the slummiest part of Holborn.

Where the Prudential rears its clifflike front – a terra cotta New Jerusalem – there at the back is Brooke's Market, an ideal place to dream awhile, to lounge of a summer evening under the plane trees or to feed its pigeons, some of the most corpulent in town. I truly believe that the installation of parking meters is the only event that the place has known since the most recent of its buildings went up in 1914. Once in a while you will see a tradesman from Leather Lane trundle his barrow or an old woman settle herself on a bench with a newspaper and eat something out of a bag, but that is all; usually the pigeons and the squabbling sparrows have it all to themselves. But it was not always so. Apart from the ancient tragedy of Lord Brooke, there was another, singularly pathetic, the death by suicide of the wonderful boy poet, Chatterton. I had a most interesting letter from a reader of these my occasional papers who wrote: 'I wonder if you know that the boy poet, Chatterton, starved to death in the garret of the last house in Brooke Street, which forms one side of the square. The house is at a right angle to St Alban's Church, and as I remember it was entered by a door round the corner in a little alleyway. I remember all this because I was a "Pru" girl from 1916 to 1925. This house was used by them for storage of dockets, and if we needed to refer to any of these, we would say Oh! it's over in Chatterton House, and many a time I have been up in that attic, looking out of the window, just as depicted in the famous picture by Henry Wallis, *The Death of Chatterton*.'

I should have thought myself that Chatterton's lodging disappeared somewhat before the period mentioned by my correspondent, but however this may be, the painting by Henry Wallis in the Tate Gallery is, besides being unforgettable, certainly authentic, for the background was painted in the actual attic of No. 39 Brooke Street, where the seventeen-year-old poet poisoned himself with arsenic on August 24th, 1770 (the house being then No. 4) – one of the saddest of the many who hoped to find fame in London, and instead found nothing but chill neglect and soul-destroying obscurity.

Nor is this all: some of the Cato Street conspirators lived close to Brooke's Market, and met in a room of the White Hart there in 1819; Hart Yard still exists on the west side of the market. What is more, Brooke's Market has a distinctly foreign flavour – say, that of some faded square in one of the old working-class quarters of Paris, and, like Paris, it has its mysteries. A few weeks ago, I found there a large and well preserved canvas bag, open at the top. Inside the bag was a cup and saucer, knife and fork – the real thing – none of your plastic substitutes; there was also a plate and on it a half-eaten chicken, potatoes and greens to match – abandoned by persons unknown, like the Marie Celeste, and as mysterious. A Maupassant would have seen a little story in it, bitter sweet, well cut, inconclusive: Elia, a whimsical, good tempered essay. But lacking the genius of either I was obliged to content myself by fishing out the sliced bread that accompanied the repast, presenting it to the hopeful pigeons and passing on.

Also the market has its architectural qualities. From Brooke Street you will see through the trees the clergy house of St Alban the Martyr, designed by the great artist, William Butterfield. It and the church tower – the church was damaged during the war and rebuilt, though not, unfortunately, to Butterfield's design – are all that now remains here of this most splendid example of his genius. One knows not what to admire most – the grouping of the various Gothic elements, simple and yet varied, domestic yet ecclesiastic, into a subtle whole – the colour scheme, cunningly arranged, of the facade, its bands of dull red and blue patterning the broken yellows, ochres and yellow greys of the brickwork – the ironwork of gate and lamp, which ought to be lovingly preserved – or the audacity with which Butterfield has run the mouldings of the arch starkly into the imposts, cutting them off brutally, as if he had tired of them. Butterfield, an innovator in form, was to a large extent a traditionalist in materials, and knew how to gain his effects by an adroit use of the most common, if need be.

The clergy house of St Alban's should be studied in connection with the former parsonage of St Michael's, Burleigh Street – the latter from the skill with which the architect has overcome and, indeed, turned to account the difficulties arising from a cramped and sloping site, arranged his fenestration and proportioned his masses of brickwork so as to attain the maximum variety without restlessness and finally set a small piece of sculpture, the figure of the archangel Michael, placed with such justness, such *suavitur in modo* that the satisfaction Butterfield must have taken in his artistry communicates itself freshly to us over a century of time.

A further example of the care he took in his detailing is in the courtyard of St Alban's, through the gate – the grey little courtyard with the della Robbia-style Madonna – a gas bracket, as it was when originally designed, full of grace and vitality, in wrought iron. And, if this is not enough, there is the great saddleback tower quite undamaged, a tower that only Butterfield had the nerve and authority to determine, with tracery and lancet windows that only he could design. The atmosphere of the magnificent 1860s is so strong that I sometimes feel I shall go mad with longing as I look at it, feel the need to sink my teeth into the ironwork or brickwork, to be in physical contact with it somehow. I was leaning against the lamp with my eyes shut, day-dreaming of Ruskin and Butterfield and the Pre-Raphaelites, making believe I was an earnest young curate with mutton chop whiskers, extreme ritualistic tendencies and terrible doubts about the Divine inspiration of certain portions of Holy Writ, when a woman came up and asked me if I were all right. It is distressing to have one's castles in the air so rudely broken into, even with good intent. I said, 'Yes, I was merely thinking that this clergy-house is good enough to eat.' Her rapid exit across the square was the only time I have seen a really active human being in Brooke's Market.

THE LAMB, LAMBS CONDUIT STREET

Off to the Pub

Apart from seaside resorts such as Blackpool, there are few creations of the Victorians more satisfactory than the full-blown, plushy, mirror-bedecked, Victorian pub, found at its best in London and other large cities and towns. It is a hybrid born of a marriage between the now extinct gin palace, characterised by saucy wenches, gilding, gaslight and a long bar for upright dram-drinking, and the small urban alehouse, wainscotted and divided into simple bars, a type that still remains in such examples as the delightfully unspoilt Holly Bush in Hampstead. Somewhere about the 1850s, the features of the two were combined to form the typical Victorian pub, how or by whom is not recorded: the credit must go to some unknown genius. Although endlessly varied, its basic characteristics consist of a central bar counter with surrounding drinking spaces, divided into bars of varied comfort and elaboration, and the richly carved bar fitting often terminating in a clock and arranged for the display of bottles and porcelain spirit containers. The public bar, originally patronised by the working man, paid little or no attention to decoration – one had to look across the pub for that: plain furniture and a sanded floor were its chief luxuries. Such a bar survived until quite recent years at the Museum Tavern, Great Russell Street; it has now been incorporated into a general saloon bar – the working man, presumably, having become extinct in the area. Vast sums of money were lavished on the saloon bar, the landlord's pride and joy. It was usually approached by a private entry, a narrow passage lined with tiled pictures and often with a mosaic floor. Inside, mid and late Victorian craftsmanship reached splendid, opulent heights, especially in the bar fitting, of mahogany and employing a variety of Renaissance motifs that only the Victorians could so joyously heap together: an altar to Bacchus. Nothing suggestive of taste or refinement gets a look-in, fortunately. The hallucinatory effect is heightened by the embossed, painted or gilded mirrors, sometimes purely decorative or else carrying advertisements for stout or whisky, which decorate the walls. These reflect the customers in momentary, dissolving impressions of movement and light, as well as other parts of the pub – cast iron columns, aspidistras or artificial flowers. Many Victorian pubs in London have been spoiled either by being made too Victorian in recent years (a faking that is always painful to the fancier) or otherwise by being turned into that chamber of horrors, the 'theme' pub.

Here is a handful of choice examples for the pub-crawling connoisseur, with comments:

1. The Lamb, Lambs Conduit Street, Bloomsbury.

Spendid interior – cast iron columns, original tables, theatrical photographs and snob screens. These screens were to ensure privacy for the customers of the saloon or private bars, and are now a rarity.

2. The Princess Louise, High Holborn.

Quite undamaged. A perfect example. Tiles, fireplaces, stained glass, unspoiled gents' lavatory with slate handbasins and a notice in gold letters with a hand pointing how to get there.

3. The Camden Head, Camden Passage, Islington.

Recently done up a little, but retaining its superb engraved windows with birds, flowers and plants in a rococo framework. Stained glass panels in rooms above. Very characteristic of its period, 1899. Exterior also good.

4. The Red Lion, Duke of York Street, St. James's.

Small but perfect specimen. A hall of mirrors, all set in semi-circular headed panels, and a plain mahogany bar for contrast. The mirrors, delicately engraved, are the very summit of Victorian craftsmanship in 'brilliant' glass. Clerkenwell and Kennington are two areas where this work was carried on. Even without alcohol, one imagines oneself in the boudoir of some particularly opulent, *fin de siècle* courtesan.

5. The Salisbury, St Martins Lane.

Once it was only the customers who spoiled a fantastically rich interior of this kind – they were wrongly dressed. But with sideburns and heavy moustaches again in fashion, the whole thing is back to the naughty nineties. Examine the constant nymphs holding electric lights, the brass, the marble, mahogany and plush and the views of heads reflected in mirrors.

Somewhere farther afield are:

6. The Hat and Feathers, at the corner of Goswell Road on the edge of the City.

Engraved glass, Classical figures in compo on the facade.

7. The Chippenham, near Cambridge Road, Kilburn.

Large speciment of late Victorian pub, especially interesting for its tiled decorations.

8. The Barrack Tavern.

Late Victorian pub facing Woolwich Common. It has elaborate Lincrusta ceilings and deep moulded cornice with figures of women ending in arabesques. There is also a large panel of a floating female figure, half Greek, half ship's figurehead in style, bearing a scroll with the magic words 'Bass Pale and Burton Ales' – a message from the Gods.

Old Clo'

Of course, there are old clo' and old clo' – the latter being more correctly styled period costume, much sought after nowadays and priced commensurately. There is money in both kinds. I had once a very distant relative who started out in life with nothing but a certain native flair and ambition. She married a tram driver who had aspirations far beyond his profession, and thought lavender kid gloves more to his taste than tram-driver's gloves. Together they set up a wardrobe dealer's, and lo! in the fullness of time, they prospered, became noted for the quality of their secondhand furs (of the finest French workmanship, you understand – none of your English dyed rabbit lined with crepe de chine), married their daughter to a rich man and from this came in turn a villa – in Nice I think it was: at any rate, all out of old clo'. Which just proved their potential.

I have myself dabbled in old clo' – not the kind you used to rummage for at the departed Lou's in Camden Passage, in a scrum of mothers and mothers-to-be – very much to be, some of them – and perhaps, if you weren't trampled to death, coming up with a Victorian thunder and lightning waistcoat for a bob: but like those I have acquired – two greatcoats belonging to one of King Edward VII's physicians, for instance, pleated, buttoned at the back and with dramatic velvet collars – old clothes like Queenie sells, or perhaps prefers to keep.

For Queenie Gascoigne is an original, one of the few left in London. She deals in period costumes simply because she loves them, and has at length realised her ambition to sell them from her own home to people who also care about old and beautiful clothes. Not that there is anything arty about her. Far from it. She has the good old London working-class background not too far behind and much uncommon sense, besides an impressive knowledge of clothes and when and how they would be worn and with what accessories. I have always felt that old clothes worn by people now in the grave are infinitely sad, as old toys:

> The tiny blue shoes
> That no little feet use
> Whose sight makes the fond tears start.

But it is not so to Queenie, who has a connoisseur's interest in velvety and satiny textures, the cut of a walking-out cape, the beads of a dress of the Roaring Twenties, the stitching of silk lining. All these things are beautifully renovated before Queenie, in her personal, casual way, decides to part with them – if she likes you well enough, that is.

At the time I made the accompanying drawing of Queenie's shop in Essex Road, she had on display in the window to the extreme left a superb afternoon dress of cream satin and pearls, which belonged to Lily Langtry. I had always imagined her as a statuesque Edwardian beauty, but the dress disproved it, and anyway Queenie gave it as her considered opinion that the Jersey Lily was not, in fact, beautiful, and that the attraction to the naughty King Edward lay largely in her vivacity and wit. But old clo', like certain scents, are powerfully evocative, stir memory or create vivid pictures in the mind with that sharp-edged poignancy that is experienced when the past is suddenly disturbed. Just as the 'Nimrod' of Elgar's *Enigma Variations* conveys occultly the feeling of golden Edwardian afternoons on the Malvern Hills – the musical equivalent of certain landscapes also of the period by Wilson Steer – so the creamy satin dress embroidered with lace was eloquent of tea parties on lawns of emerald grass, of carriage drives in the Park, of shopping expeditions at exclusive Bond Street establishments, of Goodwood and private views at Burlington House, of the wonderful motor car, of the magnificent men in their flying machines and of the feeling that the starchy, stuffy Victorian age was passed and that the sunlit, chocolate cream future held nothing but progress – might indeed have done so, but for the inconvenient fact that the nephew whom King Edward so rightly distrusted was nursing his hatreds and cultivating his madnesses in far away Potsdam, assisted by a few other lunatics in other high places in Europe.

'Come over here, boys, you're wanted'

'Feed the guns. Pile up the munitions'

'To dress extravagantly in war time is worse than bad taste. It is unpatriotic.'

I have no doubt that Diana of the Uplands – the most perfect type of Edwardian ideal, as seen in Furse's painting at the Tate – joined one of the women's organisations of the hideous initials and took to a chase of another sort, that of the unspeakable Hun.

'Come upstairs', said Queenie, 'and have some tea – china tea.'

There is nothing to beat china tea served in China's earth when you have been pondering overmuch on the significance of old clo'.

Queenie' 406
Essex Road Islington

QUEENIE'S, ISLINGTON

ST PETER VAUXHALL

Down Vauxhall Way

The Spring evening was unusually mild and inviting – just right, I thought, for Vauxhall, an area on which the great ones seldom let the light of their countenances shine, one that the sensation seekers but rarely penetrate. The moment was propitious. Almost immediately I came across an old man sitting on a weekly payments armchair in the centre of a vacant lot, where once some Georgian houses stood. In appearance a compound of White Knight and Billy Bennett, he told me he went there to escape his daughter-in-law and to meditate on the great times of the blackout. He remembered utility furniture coming in, and then it was the ground-nuts, and on one occasion, though only briefly, he saw Herbert Morrison. I said his life had been crowded with incident.

Vauxhall, like the rest of Lambeth, came out best, he told me, at Coronations, all bunting and Union Jacks, and I agreed, remembering a certain surgical shop there in 1953, where they had the Queen's portrait in the window, surrounded by rupture belts. I recognised him as a symbol – though of what I was unable precisely to determine – and was grateful to him for giving me that touch of melancholy I like to have on a London perambulation.

Vauxhall, bounded on the north by Black Prince Road, by the western end of the Oval to the east, by Miles Street and Fentiman Road to the south and the river to the west, takes its name from Falkes de Breauté. He was an unscrupulous Norman adventurer – rather after the style of Longfellow's Norman baron. The manor in which he lived became known as Faukeshale, which changed through many variations to end up as Vauxhall. Though there are no longer daffodils from Chelsea or violets sent from Kew to be seen there on a summer morning (unless the New Covent Garden brings them again), Vauxhall is full of interest – a place of early industrial sites, dining rooms and Gothic Revival churches. One of the finest churches is St Peter Vauxhall in Kennington Lane, built by J. L. Pearson in 1863, with adjoining school buildings – a striking and original design not unmixed with French influence. Its notable features include a deep apse decorated below the triforium stage with murals – now darkened by time – surrounding a detached altar of alabaster and mosaic, the uncusped windows, the magnificent groined vaulting of brick with stone ribs and the capitals of the nave arcade. The west front and narthex from the road forms an irregular interesting composition, marred only at close quarters by the tympani over the doors, which were left uncarved.

If you want to know where the famed Vauxhall Gardens were, you are on the door-step, St Oswald's Place, running alongside St Peter's, being one of its boundaries, the others being Kennington Lane, Vauxhall and Leopold Walks and Goding Street. Unlike Cremorne, one of whose trees remains, nothing is left of that place of frolic and fireworks, trees and tightropes, of amours in arbours. Where music and the monster ballroom entertained the Londoners of Dr Johnson's time are grisly L.C.C. flats, though the gardens had vanished long before they had arrived; had degenerated into something third rate and frowsy, as described by Dickens in the *Sketches by Boz*.

There are classic as well as gothic remains in Vauxhall – some hiding furtively behind tacked-on shops, others still unspoiled, such as the Soane style, neo-Greek villa next to St Anne's Roman Catholic Church and Brunswick House, where one of my *Daily Telegraph* readers remembers the Christmas parties held in the ballroom by the family who lived there above their place of business in the old London style.

Generally, Vauxhall's elegant days were over by the 1840s. Its final magnificent flowering is represented by a building that belongs spiritually to St Leonard's or Brighton – the Licensed Victuallers' School next to the Georgian terrace now at last being restored in Kennington Lane. This splendid facade dates from 1836. The Victuallers left for Slough in 1921, and the place was taken over by the NAAFI; it is now called Imperial Court. Charles Dickens reported the ceremony of laying the foundation stone for his newspaper, *The Morning Chronicle*, some five weeks before the appearance of the *Pickwick Papers*.

These are only a few of the sights, just to tempt you into hiring a sedan chair. And if the old man with the lemon yellow moustache is still musing on the vacant lot, you can ask him more about the blackout and the groundnuts.

Camberwell Beauty

When I heard that plans were being prepared to turn part of Sir Gilbert Scott's church of St Giles at Camberwell into a community centre, with the notion that people might meet there for social gatherings, concerts and the like, as well as for religious services, I decided it was high time to spend a couple of days there, largely to study the east window, a great rarity being designed by John Ruskin. I wanted to contemplate it in the setting which as yet remains much as Ruskin knew it. Not that there is anything special about St Giles, built between 1841–3 – down-and-outs in the porch waiting for the crypt to open and kids cycling – though the five bay nave arcade has rather fine and well proportioned piers, alternately round and octagonal on plan. The exterior, of Sneaton stone with Caen stone dressings, is on the whole the most effective part of the design, which may fairly be described as judicious, rather than as inspiring enthusiasm – typical of Scott's manufacture, except on the rare occasions when he rose above his natural pedestrianism as in St Mark's, Worsley, Lancashire. Scott always appears to me to be of the worst type of academic – as Reynolds is of the best. It would be difficult to account for his taking up Gothic forms as a means of expression at all, but for the fact that the phenomenon of romantic art in combination with fundamental worldliness is met with in other nineteenth-century artists – Delacroix, Turner and William Morris, for instance. But these contrived to keep the visionary elements apart from the practical which Scott apparently could not – the solitary exception being, of all things, St Pancras Station – hence the curious flavourlessness and orthodoxy of his work.

Eastlake, after praising the spire and criticising the fittings of the interior, goes on to remark: 'The decorative carving in the capitals etc. of St Giles's Church is better in design than execution, being coarsely cut in parts. Yet in these and other details, the work showed a decided advance in operative skill. The stained glass window at the west end, though open to objection in the style of drawing, caught something of the tone of old glass.'

Eastlake must mean the east window, the west being largely white glass in lozenge panels, surrounding a little heraldry; at any rate, he appears unaware of Ruskin's authorship of the five light east window. It is undoubtedly the most remarkable feature of the interior, doubly remarkable when we think of his youth (he was only twenty-five when he designed it with the collaboration of his friend, Edmund Oldfield) and the poor state of English glass at the time. The tracery in the window head was the first to be designed and filled – the five vertical lights came later, after Ruskin had made a close study of medieval French glass at Rouen, Chartres and Auxerre and sent to Oldfield, as E. T. Cook says, 'a constant stream of designs, suggestions and criticisms'. His letters of this time show not only the pains he took to familiarise himself with the characteristics and technicalities of old glass, but also his acute powers of observation and analysis, even to those accidental felicities of broken or variegated colour given to the glass by rust or the staining from the putties. The result of all this is a window very rich and jewel-like – admittedly a trifle brighter than ancient glass – in which several shades of ultramarine and cobalt and various crimsons predominate, together with smaller accents of greens and yellows and points of white. The effect, however, is somewhat spoiled by the light colour of the recent distemper – a light cream used not only in the chancel but also in the rest of the interior. In any country but this it would have been written up and photographed, and made the subject of Ruskinian pilgrimages, such as mine, or perhaps moved to a museum for greater safety, long ago.

The centre light (the widest of the five) contains five roundels of incidents in the life of Christ – the crucifixion the midmost, at the top a Christ in glory, at the base the birth of the Saviour. All the subjects, from the Old and New Testaments, are arranged in reserved panels – roundels, quatrefoils and half quatrefoils – and all are full of exquisite drawing and arrangement, as, for example, the incident in the Garden of Eden where Eve plucks a bright red apple from an emerald tree, watched by a scarlet snake, or Jacob's dream or Death on a pale horse or Herodias with the head of John the Baptist. The window is an illustrated Bible, like that other which Ruskin later interpreted so eloquently, the mosaic bible of St Mark's, Venice. Like it, Ruskin's window requires a considerable amount of biblical scholarship and time, if its lessons are to be learned.

Meantime the kids play football on the playground grass under the old trees behind the church, the prams go up and down Camberwell Grove, and the winos and meths men argue endlessly on the benches of the Green, for the harvest is not yet come.

ST GILES, CAMBERWELL

The Arch in the Sky

The arch in the sky was the *Rainbow*, and I read – devoured – it avidly every week, along with a veritable library of companion papers, notably those in which the charming Bruin Boys appeared – *Tiger Tim's Weekly* and *Playbox*, in which the Bruin Boys' sisters, the Hippo girls, were featured.

Therefore I read that the Fleetway House had been put on a short lease with a view to demolition with acute depression. There is nothing noteworthy architecturally about Fleetway House: it is only late Edwardian office style. But it was where Tiger Tim had his office, where he wrote his weekly letter, if not prevented by the naughty Bruin Boys, and where he edited his delectable annual, with another letter to his little readers and an ad for the *Weekly* on the reverse.

'You will find Tiger Tim, the Bruin Boys and all kinds of jolly little people in Tiger Tim's own paper every week . . . it is full of funny pictures, jolly stories, puzzles, tricks, jokes and models, so be sure to ask your newsagent to save you a copy every Thursday.'

I was mad about the Bruin Boys. I found this weekly supply inadequate, even with my system of re-reading old numbers. Eventually I hit upon the idea of teaching myself to draw them in all manner of positions, and at last became adept enough to produce, fairly easily, a very respectable imitation, to which I also wrote the stories. But there was an idiosyncrasy about my connoisseurship for comics that seems to me now very characteristic of my lifelong hatred of change. I began with *Chick's Own*, which you may recall, was edited by Uncle Dan and featured the most delightful drawings of Rupert the Chick and his friends by Arthur White. I added *Tiny Tots* on its appearance in 1927, then *Playbox* and all the Bruin Boys' papers, next the older, more old-fashioned comics such as *Puck* (1904 and very staid, reserved for the occasional purchase), *Chips* and *Comic Cuts*. But I never gave up the originals, so that by the time I was reading *The Magnet* and *Modern Boy* and the D. C. Thomson *Skipper*, *Rover* and *Adventure*, my early favourites were still being very enthusiastically bought and read.

I worked out all possible aspects of the Bruin Boys, and studied all the drawings carefully to compare details. Mrs Bruin's school was in some country town background, but as they came up to London, at least for the editing, I reasoned that the country town must be in the Home Counties. I familiarised myself with the appearance of the school, inside and out, and charted carefully the comings and goings of its visitors, such as the School Inspector, Dr Lion. I imagined that the artist, H. S. Foxwell, went down specially to draw them, but explained away the occasional inconsistencies in background by the theory that long practice had enabled him to draw them from memory, which he undulged under pressure, and so committed solecisms in details on occasions.

H. S. Foxwell's drawings of the Bruin Boys achieved a very high artistic standard in line and in colour, a decided improvement on the charming but somewhat primitive Bruin Boys drawings by their original artist, J. S. Baker, creator of the unforgettable 'Casey Court', which occupied a half-page panel in *Chips*. Nor was their appearance in the first issue of the *Rainbow* in February 1914 their first. They had already appeared in black and white with yellow overlay in *The Children's Encyclopaedia* – precisely the civilised (and civilising) publication that could be expected to launch the best-loved characters of the English children's comic. Its editor, Arthur Mee, was a man of unusual quality, who will be remembered when the power-seeking educationalists of the present day have been totally forgotten. He had an outlook compounded of humanistic and Christian values, now quite out of fashion. He understood that high knowledge was complementary to educating the heart. In the worst of times, the Great War and its aftermath, he believed in the best of things; he believed in children and in the coming time. The pity is that so much of his precious seed should have gone on stony ground. It could not be otherwise, for he failed to see that the system of compulsory education, the most outrageous attack on liberty ever conceived, was designed not to produce civilised men and women, but only puppets. Apart from the wickedness of consigning children to classrooms and the influence of teachers over whom parents have no control, the system is diabolical in that the minds of children are warped from the beginning – not only by exposing them to other children not of their choice and so conditioning them to democracy, teamwork and uniformity, but also at an early and receptive stage, playing on the natural desire to dominate by awarding miserable privileges – badges and the like – which has the effect of accustoming our unfortunate youngsters to authority and subordination, to accepting these revolting absurdities as natural and inevitable. To accept priests and clerics, to pay taxes, to accept governments, local and national, to acquiesce in the locking up of fellow creatures in prisons and lunatic asylums, to allow the exploitation of animals, to accept conscriptions and rationing or the welfare state: in a word, to knuckle under all the tyrannies that the English authoritarian can conceive or execute. Which is why the generation of children that Arthur Mee immediately addressed were gulled when adults into the war of 1939 as easily as their parents had been into that of 1914.

Arthur Mee also believed in progress and science, which I do not: but I must admit that the give-away scientific toys in the *Children's Newspaper* were remarkable for quality, even by Mee's standards. Not that I have ever heard of anyone's reading the *Children's Newspaper* beside myself. I suspect adults bought it, but that the kids read 'underground' comics. If so, they were the losers.

The work of these comic artists (so-called) belongs to a great English tradition

We have always had a genius for ephemeral and popular art. Some of the comic artists, unknown to the reading public, had talents that amounted to genius: H. S. Foxwell, J. S. Baker, Bert Thomas, Harry Rountree and Tom Browne. The last-named came from obscurity in Nottingham to a prosperous career in Blackheath, where he died from overwork, having created the immortal Weary Willie and Tired Tim of *Chips*, a series of charming watercolours of the Dutch fishing town of Volendam – where he followed Phil May – the familiar Johnny Walker figure with the top boots and quizzing glass, postcards, posters and book illustrations without number: a very great artist. Already this 'art work' (a mouldy, pejorative term, which unjustly sets it apart from other kinds of drawing and painting) is being collected in its published form; ultimately the originals will appear in the salesrooms, and will, I foresee, be preserved in a public collection not only for the benefit of students, but also for those who recognise the importance of unimportant art, and delight in it.

We could also do worse than spare a thought for that strange genius, Alfred Harmsworth, Lord Northcliffe, who made so many of these comics possible, earning immortality thereby. When the Fleetway House has gone, he will still have his memorial in the office building it was his early ambition to build in Fleet Street. It is now occupied by Messrs. Alfred Bates, advertising consultants. There are two flagpoles on the Fleet Street facade. Northcliffe's office was immediately above the lower one. There is also, of course, the actual memorial to this remarkable man who fostered such good things for children, almost as a byproduct of journalistic enterprise: the bronze head in St Dunstan's churchyard. Last time I inspected it, there was a pigeon perched there, warily eyeing the traffic preparatory to crossing Fleet Street. He blinked his little ruby eyes in mild surprise as I murmured '*Nisi monumentum requiris, circumspice*', and then flapped his beautiful wings and flew away.